THE OTHER SIDE OF SORROW

The
Other Side
of
Sorrow

Poets Speak Out about
Conflict, War, and Peace

Patricia Frisella
Editor

Cicely Buckley
Associate Editor

POETRY SOCIETY OF NEW HAMPSHIRE

ISBN-13: 978-0-9724167-1-9
ISBN-10: 0-9724167-1-4

Library of Congress Control Number: 2006900426

Designed and composed in Fournier MT
at Hobblebush Books, Brookline, New Hampshire
(www.hobblebush.com)

Printed in the United States of America

Published by:

POETRY SOCIETY OF NEW HAMPSHIRE

31 Reservoir Road · Farmington New Hampshire 03835

*Books may be ordered from the Poetry Society at this address,
or by e-mail at* frisella@worldpath.net

To all those who honor the fallen
by working for a lasting peace

Acknowledgments

This book was made possible by grants from the following:

The New Hampshire Charitable Foundation
The Samuel P Hunt Foundation
The Anne Slade Frey Charitable Trust
The Lizzie Cheney Trust, TD Banknorth, NA
The many contributors to the matching grant

I wish to thank them all for their belief in this project.

I also owe thanks to my husband and children for their patience while I worked on this manuscript. They listened to my many complaints with sympathy and love for the task at hand, offering good counsel. They were my constant companions for this journey. Also thanks to John-Michael Albert for his technical assistance, his deep knowledge, and his artistic eye. He was my rudder. Thanks to Cicely Buckley for introducing me to so many fine poets. And finally, thanks to all the poets who asked for nothing more than the chance to speak and be heard. I have the greatest respect for their heart and their work. I have read this manuscript many times and found myself overwhelmed each time by the beauty and power of their words. I hope you, too, will savor this journey.

Patricia Frisella
January, 2006

Contents

CONTENTS

CONTENTS

CONTENTS

CONTENTS

CONTENTS

THE OTHER SIDE OF SORROW

RS Thomas

Borders

Somewhere beyond time's
curve civilization lifted
its glass rim. There was
a pretense of light

for nations to walk by
through the dark wood, where history
wintered. Following I came
to the foretold frontier

where with a machine's
instinct the guns' nostrils
flared at the blooms held out
to them by the flower people.

➵

Geoffrey Chaucer

Excerpt from "Prudence and Melibeus"

TRANSLATED BY Robert Dunn

My lords, there is many a man cries, "War! War!"
that knows full little what war amounts to.
War at its beginning opens wide, that everyone may
lightly enter; but the end is not light to know.

For truly when that war is once begun
there is full many a child unborn of its mother
that shall starve young because of that same war,
or else live in sorrow and die in wretchedness.

Therefore before any war begins men must have
great counsel and deliberation.

➵

GAYLE PORTNOW

The Teamster

*After a 1916 painting by George Bellows at the
Farnsworth Museum, Rockland, Maine*

Bony ribs, naked in the light
like the colossal skeleton of a beached whale.
The ruddy teamster looks away.
Pale sun-bleached wood builds a ship
for men to die on far from home.

Twin horses burdened by the hull
wait on rocky ground, uncertain as the churning sea.
The prow, unfinished,
cuts through raging purple clouds,
a weather warning of impending war.

→►

GAYLE PORTNOW

A Time of War

*After a 1941 painting by Carol Thayer Berry, at the
Farnsworth Museum, Rockland, Maine*

If war is Hell
why are we prospering?
Fiery orange-red towers stand watch
over rusty brown cranes, angled
like rocket-launchers poised to kill.
Men in blue crowd gangplanks,
crushed together, frantic,
eager, happy to be working,
building for our Second World War
as if one was not enough.

→►

LAURE-ANNE BOSSELAAR

The Feather at Breendonk

I am praying again, God — pale God —
here, between white sky and snow, by the larch
I planted last spring, with one branch broken at the elbow.
I pick it up, wave winter away, I do things like that,
call the bluebirds back, throwing yarn and straw
in the meadow, and they do come, so terribly blue,
their strangled *teoo-teoo*

      Echoing my prayer *Dieu, Dieu* —
the same *Dieu* who stained the feather I found
in the barbed fields of the Breendonk Concentration Camp
near Antwerp in 1952. My father tried to slap it
out of my hand: *It's filthy*. But I held on to it —
I knew it was an angel's. *They only killed
a few Jews here*, he said, *seven, eight hundred, maybe.*

      So I wave their angels away with my feather,
away from my father, away from the terribly blue skies
over the Breendonk Canal, where barges loaded bricks
for Antwerp, where my father loaded ships for Rotterdam,
Bremerhaven and Hamburg — as Antwerp grew,
and the port expanded, and his business
flourished, and all the while he kept repeating:

      That's all we needed: a good war . . .

→⊱

DON KIMBALL

Seeing Our Soldiers Off

    After Thucydides, Book 6, 30–31

All, who are able, walk with them as far
as guards allow — the locals, immigrants,

all manner of people escorting those they hold
close to them, their buddies, sweethearts,
fiancés, husbands or wives, sons or daughters,
most of them confounding hope with sobs;
and where they walk, their prospects of profit, pride
or glory weighing against the likelihood
of never seeing the ones they love, again;
at last, admitting to themselves just where it is
on the global map, this noble expedition
is taking them. And now that it is here,
that painful moment of parting, duffel bags
packed full with such uncertainty, the peril
seeming more important than what it was
they thought they voted for, their resolve to battle
is barely restored by all the blare, the show
of force surrounding them. As for us,
the foreigners, the ones too old to fight,
we stay at home to reap the body count.

→►

DON KIMBALL

The Warrior's Song

For Priscilla

I am a warrior waiting for true love
to waltz his night away. Are you the woman
who knows this dance? Can hawks romance a dove?
I am a warrior waiting. Stay, my love —
do not be shy! May I remove your glove
so you might prove this war-torn heart is human?
I am a warrior waiting for true love
to waltz the night away. Are you this woman?

→►

Basic

Strut young and hard they were,
super-hero uniformed and loud
with laughter and obscenities.
Barked and bullied to a grinning
pride they wheeled and
counter marched and nightly
dreamt of an undreaming sleep.

Boyless brave and hot they were,
in a dark and noisome school
of mud; stung and creatured
to a knowledge biblical of bug
and worm carnality, gardened
in a paradise of razor wired
perimeters and buzzing serpent lies.

Joyless grave and strong they were,
and brothered close in nightwise fear
and swore themselves the enemies
of day. They stifled every gleam
and glisten, every sound of metal
music stopped and bound, every
curvature and softness looked away.

Bullet slick and mad they were,
belly sinuating in the grass and sick
to be so near the idol of their lust.
They worshipped closed up to the ass
of war and kissed it. And ever after
to the never-having-been said, No.
Of course, no. They never missed it.

→>-

MAGGIE KEMP

They Fired the Shot

Drugs slammed down to stay awake
Souls resounded, hear them quake
To kill the enemy they must stay awake
What's a few comrades to killers make?
They killed them all, shot them down . . .

They fired the shot, dropped the bomb
Lucifer sent them all around
They killed them all, shot them down . . .

Yes, sir, no, sir, good soldiers make
Sergeant Rilko, where is your stake?
I followed orders, they stayed awake
Bodies are cheap, just pick up a rake
My men, my women, they stayed awake
I followed orders, for my army's sake.

They fired the shot, dropped the bomb
Lucifer sent them all around
They killed them all, shot them down . . .

Captain Cooley, why didn't you say, It's a fake!
Our neighbors take orders from their own drake
Ask my Major, for God's sake!
Major Jake, why experiment on our fighting stake
Ask the Colonel why Marines we take.

They fired the shot, dropped the bomb
Lucifer sent them all around
They killed them all, shot them down . . .

Mister General Loewenthal
Are drugs the way to make them heed our call?
The goats ran amuck, weren't alert for our friends.
Well-regulated drugs have nothing to do with judgment
Damn the goats!

Scapegoats . . .

➻

8

PAUL NICHOLS

No Fear

NO FEAR read the tag
on his civilian shirt
and the decal
on his pickup window
Ripe with youthful illusions
fed by hungry recruiters
fresh from high school restraints
"There's a war on
gotta get me some"

Months later
gullibility stings
in a forbidding arena
Young warrior gags
on fear

Glory
mission
his role emerges
expendable
as a shear pin
when the drive wheel binds
a pawn in the shop of war

One errant move
a detonator fires
the charge explodes
jagged ingots
sear
tear
soft flesh
beneath
body armor's trust

Now a different shirt
tagged with blood
bone-white shards
where sleeves were full

Strapped to a gurney
jaw clamped tight
a morphine haze calls back
that high school psych class
the lightness of each topic
an intense understanding now
'fight or flight' means nothing
when neither is possible

➠

Hugh Harter

The Shepherd Guard

Night's shapes merged slowly and began to change.
The rocks, the trees, all seemed to sway and move,
The sea, to rise and touch the clouds now tinged with rose.
With slow deliberate pace, the sun
Had risen in the sky and day had come!
No ambush spear could drive its fatal metal
Into my heart, its marksman hidden
By the night's dark cloak. So did I think,
When suddenly I heard a noise.
I turned. There stood a youth, as frightened and surprised as I.
Transfixed, we were puppets angling on Fate's strings.
I watched him as he raised his spear,

Then held it poised and ready for the kill.
A glint of sun upon the blade half blinded me and then,
As I looked into his face again, I saw him laugh.
And as I saw him laughing there, I laughed too,
That morning in my fear, and as I laughed,
I raised my spear, as ready for the kill as he!
Before I struck, I searched his face, untouched as yet
By time or care, eyes blue, lips fragile as a girl's.
For one short moment, I saw his nostrils flair.
I caught my breath and gulped for air.
I stood transfixed before his stare,
Enthralled in ecstasy that priests must feel
Before the venomed beauty of a sacred snake.
I looked and saw my horror in those eyes,
Flayed horror in the wonder of those eyes.
My enemy, my friend, brief laughing youth,
Who found my life as I found his
Before the chambered fastnesses of death.
I was that fellow man, the very man I had to kill!
By then, I'd felt my spear twist in my hand
As blade met flesh and fused with it.
We looked into each other's eyes.

He smiled a tortured smile at me, and I at him,
He moved a step and fell toward me,
My brother, and my friend, my enemy,
Before my lips could say the single word of comfort they sought to form.
I closed his eyes, those gentle eyes, and I myself could see no more.
All that was left was darkness and the murky solitude of death!

→➤

MIMI WHITE

Zaydee's Short Career in the Russian Army

I heard a noise like feet rustling.
It was so dark you couldn't see the sky.
I said, "Halt, or I'll shoot!"
It moved closer until I felt its steamy breath.
I shot one, two, three times.
The general's cow collapsed at my feet.
Looking at it,
I thought about America,
and what a wonderful place it would be to live.

→➤

ILYA KAMINSKY

Maestro

What is memory? what makes a body glow:
an apple orchard in Moldova and the school is bombed —

when the schools are bombed, sadness is forbidden
— I write this now and I feel my body's weight:

the screaming girls, 347 voices
in the story of a doctor saving them, his hands

trapped under a wall, his granddaughter dying nearby —
she whispers *I don't want to die, I have eaten such apples.*

He touches her mouth as a blind man reading lips
and yells *Shut up! I am near the window, I*

am asking for help! Speaking,
he cannot stop speaking, in the dark:

of Brahms, Chopin he speaks to them to calm them.
A doctor, yes, whatever window

framed his life, outside: tomatoes grew, clouds passed and we
once lived. A doctor with a tattoo of a parrot on his trapped arm,

seeing his granddaughter's cheekbones
no longer her cheekbones, with surgical precision

stitches suffering and grace:
two days pass, he shouts

in his window (there is no window) when rescue
approaches, he speaks of Chopin, Chopin.

They cut off his hands, nurses say he is "doing OK"
— in my dream: he stands, feeding bread to pigeons, surrounded

by pigeons, birds on his head, his shoulder,
he shouts *You don't understand a thing!*

he is breathing himself to sleep, the city sleeps,
there is no such city.

➵

JULIA OLDER

Czechoslovakia

And while I slept
Russian soldiers marched into Prague.

Puppeteers forced peopled hands
into their pockets and wept
behind black hoods of invisibility.
Blondes no longer lifted gossamer fringed lashes
to slide a wink or two at awestruck lovers.
Radio Prague became monotonous wavelengths
forced around the globe with nothing to tell
as the Russian soldiers marched into Prague.
Children would not kiss their mothers in fear.
Music which had always been their laughter
echoed down the black tunnels of rifles
while I slept much too soundly and dreamt
of the frenzied hen who wanders
from her eggs for a kernel of corn
and returns to find them gone.

➟

TESS BAUMBERGER

The Death of American Innocence

*Written in response to people saying that 9/11
marked the death of American innocence*

Innocence does not die at once, in that first raptured thrust.
It dies in every small seduction, in every subsequent acquiescence.
American innocence did not die in that bright flashing terrorist act,
it dwindled breath by breath, in great and tiny acts of terror,

It died with every smallpox blanket sold to an Indian village,
with every arrogantly greed-wrested acre,
with every language and culture annihilated,
it died on the Trail of Tears.

It died with every African shackled and torn from homeland, family,
with every auction block sale of humanity,
with every black woman raped by a white slave owner,
it died in the Middle Passage.

13

It died with every civil rights activist beaten or killed,
with Martin Luther King, Malcolm X, and the Black Panthers
it died in Montgomery and Selma and Little Rock and Chicago.

It died with every gay, lesbian, bisexual, or transgendered person
beaten or killed because of their sexual orientation or identity.
It died with Harvey Milk and Matthew Shepard. It died at Stonewall.

It died with Roosevelt's refusal to accept Jews fleeing the Nazis,
it died with every black man sent first to the front lines
it died with two atomic weapons dropped upon Japan,
170,000 lives lost in two great flashing instants.

It dies with every chemical weapon developed,
with every nuclear test, wherever it happens,
with every bomb or jail built instead of a school.

It dies with every KKK rally and every single lynching,
with every man searched by police because he's black,
with every black man beaten by white officers,
with every child who witnesses or perpetuates gang warfare,
it dies with every racist or sexist or homophobic or anti-Semitic joke.

It dies with every bombed synagogue, mosque, temple,
with every black church burned,
with every abortion clinic bombed,
with every hate-filled word or deed.

It dies with every sweatshop built on a poorer country's soil,
with every product bought, made by a political prisoner,
with every homeless person,
with every starving despairing child.

Oh, innocence never dies at once, only delusion does.

➤➤

DUNYA MIKHAIL

Inanna

TRANSLATED BY BARBARA WINSLOW

I am Inanna.
And this is my city.
And this is our meeting
round, red and full.
Here, some time ago,
someone was asking for help
shortly before his death.
Houses were still here
with their roofs,
people,
and noise.
Palm trees
were about to whisper something to me
before they were beheaded
like some foreigners in my country.
I see my old neighbors
on the TV
running
from bombs,
sirens
and Abo Al-Tubar.
I see my new neighbors
on the sidewalks
running
for their morning exercises.
I am here
thinking of the relationship
between the mouse and the computer.
I search you on the Internet.
I distinguish you
grave by grave,
skull by skull,
bone by bone.

I see you
in my dreams.
I see the antiquities
scattered
and broken
in the museum.
My necklaces are among them.
I yell at you:
Behave, you sons of the dead!
Stop fighting
over my clothes and my gold!
How you disturb my sleep
and frighten a flock of kisses
out of my nation!
You planted pomegranates and prisons
round, red, and full.
These are your holes in my robe.
And this is our meeting . . .

➙➤

David Romtvedt

The Bells of Balangiga

Balangiga, The Philippines, late September, 1901

1.
They rang the bells and jumped
from hiding to attack the Americans.
Thirty-four men dressed as women —
heads covered, layers of extra clothes.
They carried small coffins. Why so many
women with coffins? "Please show me,"
a U.S. soldier ordered, and the woman,
opening the lid, displayed her dead child.
"Cholera," she said. The soldier
let the woman pass, the other women, too.
Inside their robes were bolos,

heavy machetes the Filipinos used
to cut cane, to clear brush. A week before,
two drunk American soldiers went into a shop
to buy tuba wine and while waiting
tried to rape the shopkeeper. She screamed
and her brothers beat up the drunks.
U.S. troops rounded up 143 men —
every male over ten years old.
They confiscated bolos and destroyed
the town's store of rice. In response,
the thirty-four men as wailing women.
One of them, Capitan Valeriano Abanador
grabbed Private Adolph Gamlin's rifle
and clubbed him. Then 500 undisguised men
rose from hiding and killed American soldiers.
The American general asked, "How many
of our men died?" Maybe forty-eight or fifty-nine
or seventy-one. No one was sure. "I want to know,"
the general said, and ordered the region pacified,
telling his troops to take no prisoners.
He said that the more Filipinos killed, the better,
the more houses burned, the better.
And tens of thousands died.
How many, no one was sure.
In these circumstances, my mother asked,
"Would you take up weapons?"

2.
When the Americans recaptured Balangiga
they took three bells. Two went to Wyoming,
to Warren Air Force Base. For a century,
the Filipinos have asked for the bells back
and the bells ring in the desert air, ring
through the smell of sage, a ship sinking
and the headlong rush to the lifeboats.
In the church above the post office the bells ring
for souls lost, souls found, souls forgotten.
There are remembered bells on winter mornings
and the girl across the street who in summer

rode her new bike around my house, ringing the bell
on her handlebar, skittering by, laughing and yelling,
"Look at my bike." And there's the bell choir,
the perfect white gloves of the players,
the Lutheran hymns, and the Jewish bakery
in Toronto where I went for my mother to buy bread.
I was in love with the baker's daughter,
nicknamed Bells. I never said it aloud
but I'd heard her father call her, "Bells."
My father told me to stay away from Jews
but I paid no mind and imagined I might say,
"A loaf of rye, please, Bells." She would turn,
surprised to hear me say her secret name
and her father with his gray hair and sweet roll
in hand would smile seeing that I loved her.
He'd waggle his finger as if to say, "Go on.
Go on," not blaming me so much for the past
through which I have lived but could not love.

➤➤

PAUL BAMBERGER

A War Story

we came upon you
body rolled into a ditch
tossed to the oblivion
of the untagged body
the talk of men is casual
where the dead carry no weight
hunker down boy
keep low boy
grab on
roots and all boy
storming coming up this hill boy
night coming up this hill boy
there are boys who travel with death slung across their backs

boys who dreamed only the glory ride of heroes
boys whose story will only be told in the return of the bones
war is a river twice crossed
I see you standing in the shade of a mango on the far bank of a river
and you are old as a church bell ringing

→→

PRISCILLA BURLINGHAM

Imprint, Tiananmen Square

The man who stood
before the tank
a wingless bird
with a giant's heart
they caged him anyway

Now we see him
through Goya's eyes
etched and inked
in black and grey

Looking back from
the curve of the world
at the body
he should have had

Moon for eye
his hand held up
to scatter tanks
like frightened sheep

No cage is large enough
for his kind
quills are forming
we have felt the boom
of his sonic heart

→→

ROBERT CORDING

Christmas Soccer Game, 1915

I suppose what made it possible
Was that no one expected more
Than a day of unhurried hours, better
Food, some free time to reread old letters,
Write new ones. Small Christmas trees
With candles lined both sides of the trenches
And marked the two days' truce.

Who can explain it? — one minute troops
Are sitting in mud, the next raising themselves
Out of the trenches, as if all they needed
Was a soccer ball to remind them
Of who they were. Imagine a Scotsman
Heading the ball into the air and catching it
On his instep, then flicking it across

The frosted grass to a German smoking
A cigarette who smiles and settles the ball,
Then boots it back. Soon a few soldiers
From both sides circle around the Scotsman
And the ball moves quickly back and forth,
Left foot, right foot, all of the men rocking
From side to side, the ball, the cold,

Making good neighbors of them all.
A game's begun, a real match without referees,
Attack and counterattacks, the ball crossing
From side to side, a match played,
We can imagine, as if it were all that mattered,
As if the game's sudden fizzes of beauty —
Three crisp passes or two perfect triangles

Laying end to end and pointing to the goal —
Could erase what they had learned
To live with. Laughing, out of breath, dizzy
With the speed of the ball skipping over

The frozen earth, did they recognize themselves
For a short while in each other? History says
Only that they exchanged chocolate and cigarettes,

Relaxed in the last ransomed sunlight.
When the night came and they had retreated
To their own sides, some of the men
Wrote about the soccer game as if they had to
Ensure the day had really happened. It did.
We have the letters, though none of them says
How, in the next short hours, they needed,

For their own well-being, to forget everything
That had happened that Christmas day.
It was cold, the long rows of candles must have
Seemed so small in the dark. Restless, awake
In the trenches, the men, I suppose,
Already knew what tomorrow would bring,
How it would be judged by the lost and missing.

→►

ALDO TAMBELLINI

once

once
　　on epiphany day
　　january 6 '44
　　at exactly 1:00 p.m.
　　we all looked at the sky
　　knowing the American b29s
　　were moving in our direction
　　we did not move
　　it was a numb fascination
　　conditioned by months of false alarms

once
>
> the bombs dropped
> destroying the neighborhood
> that was mine
> in those details contained in childhood secrets

once
>
> I saw the earth hurled by force
> in chunks lifting to the sky
> friends & neighbors died
> others survived deformed

once
>
> I heard mothers calling
> familiar names in desperation

once
>
> at the first detonation
> I jumped off the bike
> face touching my street
> lying under shattered glass falling
> walls ripped open

once
>
> is with the images on the cold screen
> that see war in their faces

that once
>
> it is not a TV show
> played for the rating

✈

KATE BARNES

Miklos Radnoti, 1909–1944

Separated from her, he saw her blue eyes in the sky,
his young wife whom he called,
"beautiful as light, beautiful as shadow."
Meanwhile, the forced march, men pissing blood,
the last beaten to death — and he among them,
one more dead man tumbled
into the common pit.

                        When his wife got there,
two years later, to identify the body,
she found a notebook still in his trenchcoat pocket,
the poems inside it growing smaller and smaller
as his strength gave way. Almost
at the end, he told about watching sheep
step into shallow water
by a lakeshore. "The rippled flock,"
he wrote, "bends to the clouds and drinks."

➻

GERTRUDE HALSTEAD

imagine you

imagine   you
on another continent
hot and humid winds
carry staccato sounds
       of fire
            you run
you hide
            you tunnel
to the shrill
of sirens
not those Ulysses heard

➻

GERTRUDE HALSTEAD

question

where were you
when they herded us
black boots and flames
where were you
when tears and prayer
parted the seas
for only a few

➤

GERTRUDE HALSTEAD

i stand on the first mountain looking east

that year   budding stopped
doorknobs held hands prisoner
numbed we sat close
hail drummed our eyelids
on nightmares
we entered ovens
sifting ashes

➤

DAVID CONNOLLY

On the Bien Hoa Berm

2200 Hours
Two Hours in Country

The first firing was down to our left,
a rumbling rattle
that flowed and ebbed
and then suddenly died
with two single shots
and a wailing scream
that left us all wide-eyed.

The FNG next to me
said it was a "gook."
Another said
it was definitely American,
like any of us has a clue.

There was more firing,
more screams,
through that night,
the next day,
the whole tour.

I learned to tell who was shooting
by the sound of their weapons,
but never could tell
who was dying
by the sound of their voices.

→-

RODGER MARTIN

Xóm Bào Dón

In the year of the spiraling dragon, squads
of muddy soldiers flummoxed five-tons
through abandoned landscapes of deepening, end-
of-rainy-season day. They rattled past
the rusted bulk of an APC stripped of all

but its burned-out shell. It lay
half submerged in a paddy; the rosette
of a rocket grenade that didn't get through
splattered next to the melted hole
that did. Later, at an intersection of dikes,

trees rose — verdant, level, a dry oasis.
They revved their engines down, dismounted,
examined this almost island. Two palms,
a banana tree, some fruits at one end,
tall bushes at the other. In the center,

a raised rectangle of baked earth. At the far
end of that pad, a low mound
of hard, blackened clay. Farther

across the paddies lay the deadly line
of The Boi Loi Woods. The Hobo Woods

that tomorrow they'll splinter and plow under.
Tonight, this island will keep them dry. The mystery
of the Phouc-Uh cried, whether bird or lizard,
it hid within the bosk. They dug foxholes,
discoursed over the mound. One thought it altar —

pagan's place for worship. Another, like
concrete they poured for hootches at camp.
They admired its hardness. The moon reflected
in the paddies. Then, one found a flake
of charred wood; this had been foundation.

The altar — a hearth for mother, a daughter, sister.
Chickens once clucked among the bushes.
Muffled night groans of a tethered water buffalo
had echoed beneath the fronds and canopy of stars.
The Phouc-Uh called again through the darkness.

JACK HALEY

Don't Count

My machine gun malfunctions
I have a run away gun
I have to break the belt feeder
100 rounds
locked and loaded
can't break the belt
can't cut the ties.
My K-bar knife hangs off my hip
my machine gun rests on my shoulder,
fires hysterically
like a demon
like the finger of God.

Smoke clouds my eyes
blinded by the silence
finally a corpsman hollers
2 wounded, 1 dead

JACK HALEY

Con Thien

Converging
out of the corner
of my eye

I see myself
pull back
the slide
and squeeze
the trigger.
You can do that
with a 45.
I have no problem
with that.
It's just the sound
that I would hear
from behind me,
that gurgling sound,
of someone drowning
in their own blood,
that still grabs me
by the windpipe
while I'm clearing
my throat at night.

—→—

MICHAEL CASEY

a bummer

we were going single file
through his rice paddies
and the farmer
started hitting the lead track
with a rake
he wouldn't stop
the track commander went
to talk to him
and the farmer
tried to hit him too
so the tracks went sideways

side by side
through the guy's fields
instead of single file
Hard On, Proud Mary
Bummer, Wallace, Rosemary's Baby
The Rutgers Roadrunner
and Go Get Em — Done Got Em
went side by side
through the fields
if you have a farm in Vietnam
and a house in hell
sell the farm
and go home

-►-

MICHAEL CASEY

people parts

why is the shit not burned?
long story   sir
I ask you where are the gloves
used to move the shit cans
well you have to ask Sergeant Young
that very same question
he took the gloves to the ville
to move the people parts
dead persons formerly beings
from the middle of the road
said it was a road obstruction
he never returned them
to where they was
the way they were   sir

-►-

LEE SHARKEY

Eye Problems

A rubber-coated metal bullet struck Ziad's eye during clashes in Bethlehem. . . .
His eyeball fell in the palm of his hand and his friends say he kept holding it till
he reached the hospital. He thought they could put it back in.
    — Muna Hamzeh, *Refugees in Our Own Land*

What do you do with an eye in the cup of your hand?

What do you see that you didn't?

What do you make of a sphere of jelly with fins of torn muscle?

What do your fingers impress on the rind?

Do you rush it to hospital, where a surgeon waits to fuse sight to vision?

Does the eye have a nationality? A history?

Does the eye have a user name?

Its own rubber bullet?

Where is the eye transcribed?

An anablep's pupil has two parts. The upper sees in air, the lower in water

A little globe there and you are the keeper

Of the watery anteroom, of the drink of clear glass

Dear eye

Once it lay snug in fat in its orbit

Once it saw as a child

Through humor a peppering of stars

→⤐

Jenin, Palestine

I don't see an old man
eyes watery like my grandfather's
when I shoot your foot, your hand
I see intolerable resistance

I don't see a pregnant woman
walking hand on hip like my sister-in-law
when I target your steps with my rifle
I see a breeder of vermin

I don't see a home
cozy, cluttered rooms like my mother's house
when I topple walls with my bulldozer
I see a nest of suicide bombers

My cousin will not hesitate to ride the bus
My daughter will not avoid sidewalk cafes
We will crush terror with fear
We will guarantee safety with annihilation

My family, my nation will survive
Some causes are worth killing for —
I would sacrifice my own life . . .

Marrakesh (Morocco), 1880

*Declare war upon those to whom the Scriptures were revealed but believe
neither in God nor in the Last Day, and who do not forbid that which God
and his Apostles have forbidden, and who refuse the true religion, until they
pay the poll-tax without reservation and are totally subjugated.*

— The Koran, 9.29–30

Nailed to the ground, I see only
the sweat-darkened fetlock of your horse,
still more graceful than the foot of my mule.

Blood washes away the taste of my
servant's mint tea — I recall her downcast eyes
as she took her wages and that bit of stew.
We eat little at our age, my wife and I.

A child shrieks — I remember my servant's son,
so small, though the eldest, carefully wiping our step.
Blood spatters into my eyes, my ears ring.

I welcome the darkness, the absence of sound,
like our silent praying in the bare synagogue
beneath the unpatched roof.

Your blows now indistinguishable
as the unmarked graves
concealing our dead from your desecrations.

However little could be left of me,
ransoming my corpse will impoverish my wife.
If only I could tell her to leave me for the dogs.

➵

Jerusalem, Aug. 10, 2001

Rabbis rush out into blood-
splashed streets in white gloves
picking up pieces
from the sidewalks
and dusty hoods of dented cars.

A hand, a toe, a nose.

For to rest in peace
one must be buried whole.

A child, her tears thinning
the blood on her cheeks,
stumbles over bodies, calling out
to her mother and when she finds her
she cannot fathom why her mother will not rise,
take her hand and lead her away.

A man bleeds from a gap
between his legs as he begs
for help from a soldier
who's really just a boy in uniform.

The boy throws down his gun
vomits not just the breakfast
his mother made him that morning.

Will the rabbis see this and rush over,
pick up with their white gloves
the tenderness of this boy splashed
on the sidewalk and put it back
inside him so he can be whole again?

➳

John-Michael Albert

The Best Fish

The best fish I ever ate was pulled
from the Gulf of Aquaba, alive,
and boiled in oil right there, on the beach.
Not gutted. Not scaled. Not beheaded.
Just crack the skin anywhere,
my eager hosts said, *and dig*
the sweet, white meat
from under the crust of skin and scales.

     Ali Reza and his best friend stand guard
     together. Smoking. Talking quietly
     about their plans for when they get out.
     The Savak, the Iranian Secret Police,
     pull up in a jeep, wrestle a burlap bag
     over Ali's best friend's head, throw him
     into the back of the jeep, and screech away.

There was nothing to be said, Ali told me,
deep in memory. *He was gone. He wasn't*
seen again. His name can't even be
mentioned in his parents' home. And I'm
afraid I know what happened to him:

The CIA taught the Savak to tie a detainee's
arms behind him at the elbows and the thumbs;
to hang him by block-and-tackle from the roof beams;
to lower him, stripped and shamed, into boiling oil.
First his feet, then his calves begin to blister
and crackle. And the truth, any truth, really,
will flow from him like tears.

                                         →-

JIM IRONS

U.S. Attacks Wedding Party

The groom was a terrorist,
and the best man
had been shooting a rifle.

The bridesmaids
were giggling like bridesmaids
everywhere,

but the bride herself
might have been wearing
a suicide bomb.

Bodies were wrapped in blankets
after the attack:

15 children,
10 women,
carried from the safe house.

You can't blame the pilot.
You never know
when it's hostile fire

or someone celebrating a wedding.

→→

MICKEY CESAR

trenches

Sacraments have a different smell
here where the topsoil sinks deep,
and mud claims every living thing:
sludge, detritus, the silk of spiders
and all things hidden from the sun;

mold-touched sheets of Leviticus,
the taste of copper in water,
the scent of sisters too long in the attic,
oak leaves, grubs, all stop
at the water's edge.

For long stretches
God is unwilling to bend:
beyond lay dry seas,
scorched bitterness,
scorpions the taste of crushed bone:
steam-dried roasted petroleum.

→►

MARJORY HEATH WENTWORTH

Linthong

We are the foam
floating on a vast ocean.
We are the dust
wandering in endless space.
Our cries are lost
in the howling wind.
— Unknown Vietnamese Refugee

1.
Waiting in the JFK IMMIGRATION LINE
Linthong drinks from a metal fountain.
Water circles in the back of his throat.

He opens his plastic bag for inspection:
one comb, a pair of Levis, and a knife.

2.
Swimming across
the Mekong River
open knife clenched
between his teeth

rope twisted
around the waist
of his sister
beside him
pulled under
ducking beneath
the moonlight
he dragged her
to a fishing boat
in the South China Sea

For weeks
they sailed with rice sacks
rigged to the mast
until a typhoon whipped
the cracked cotton to shreds
and pulled his sister
into the eager water
when the winds died
they burned planks
torn from the deck
boiled sea water to
catch steam in a tube
drops on the tongue

3.
In the Philippino camp,
ribs lined up
on his chest like a xylophone,
he learned English in the morning
and sold black market cigarettes
in the afternoon. Before he could sleep
he said the words milk and highway,
because he like the sound.
He dreamed of California,
but he lives in Salem, Massachusetts
in two rooms with eleven other people.
Every morning he goes to school
while the Lao fishermen take buses

37

to Gloucester to pack
fish into ice at the Gortons Factory.

And the women stay behind
sorting light bulbs, batteries,
and sneakers in the refrigerator,
leaving cooked rice and milk
in uncovered bowls on the cupboard.

4.
On Sundays Linthong chases sandpipers
in and out of the tide, pulsing
along the length of Singing Beach.
Dozens of spinnakers dot the horizon
like strange beautiful balloons.

He sits on a barnacled log,
tugs seaweed loose and chews.
Sucking on drops of ocean,
he watches fishermen
cast clear lines to the sea.

➻

BECCA KRASNER

Tracks

I.
The train to Lyon is blue
and dirty. The headrests smell of stale sweat,
the ashtrays overflow with empty
cigarette packs. Two girls escape
to the smoking car with cigarettes rolled with hash.
The boys read Glamour and Maxim.
The gentle sway of the train
is sea-sickening.

In Strasbourg, the houses are Tudor;
red geraniums explode from black

and white window boxes. We squeeze
into the cramped youth hostel,
cleaner than the one in Wales where,
we learn, the English students in our sister program
awoke to find crabs nesting
in their skin.
In the graffitied lobby, between drunken Danish tourists,
the president's face hovers luminous
on the TV screen. Flags flicker across the map,
each one more troops deployed. In France,
it is legal to show death
in real time.

2.

The average French tram driver knows
the bone-on-metal scream of one suicide
before he retires. The tram in Strasbourg tells us:
Attention à la fermature des ports.
We argue war and peace. I am alone to fight
the fighting, while twelve other heads shake
without question. The singsong, automated voice
is shrill and accurate; one must
mind the closed doors
as much as any other barrier.

3.

The Paris airport is paned
and arching, patrolled by machine guns.
Our flight is delayed, as it was three and a half months ago.
There has been no improvement.

We buy Jordan almonds in a bookstore for forty francs.
Sweet pastels glaze the nuts' starchy bitterness.
The cold grey of European winter seeps through the glass;
under the dull electronic hum
we no longer argue
with peace.

✈

MAXINE KUMIN

Please Pay Attention As the Ethics Have Changed
— Tag line, New Yorker *cartoon, May 10, 2004, p. 108*

Four hundred and seventeen pen-raised pheasants
were rattled — think stick

on a picket fence — into flight
for the Vice President's gun. And after that

hundreds of pen-reared mallards
were whooshed

up to be killed
by, among others, a Supreme Court Justice

statistics provided by HSUS —
the Humane Society of the United States.

The exact number of ducks, however, is wanting —
this is canned hunting

where you don't stay to pluck the feathers, pull
the innards out. Fuck

all of that. You don't do shit
except shoot.

But where is the other Humane Society, the one with rules
we used to read aloud in school

the one that takes away your license to collar
and leash a naked prisoner

the one that forbids you to sodomize
a detainee before the cold eyes

of your fellow MPs?
When the pixie soldier says cheese

for the camera who says *please pay attention?*
The ethics have changed.

Fuck the Geneva Conventions.

⤙⤚

ANNALIESE JAKIMIDES

From This September Day

All war, under law, will from this September day
on a dirt road in northern Maine where
Albertine Cyr flies her French mourning hands
into the night, often into the day, be conducted by women.
The sucklers will choose where to place the charge,
whose child to take, and what reason is good enough to send
Otto Schroeder's daughter, Muzah Bozieh's brother,
Albertine's youngest son into the fire.

She enters the room where her Freddie slept,
palms the feathered pillow's sack, the one
that rubbed his night cheeks.
Experienced witness to vulnerability,
spooner and changer, cradler of whole bodies,
her big heart swells in the cramped air
of this dark curled into its own cell.
Cap on the dresser. Church shoes by the bed.
Red fishing jacket on the doorknob.

She bruises a war cry from her tongue to slash
bayonet, napalm, missile from her vocabulary,
and smoke shadow-writing up from the merciless
shine of bones onto the moony walls: *blood, Earth,
broken hearts, supple hands, hunger, a milky mother,
hope, and open-mouthed bass in the morning.*

→＞

Thermogenesis

I.

We dance to the song of Eve,
Eve of the garden, young,
Eve in a Paradise soon to be gone,
Adam, young and vigorous, still
Virgin in his body and his mind,
Ready for rape by the apple tree.

Angels spread wings, poised for flights,
Arms raised high with bright flaming swords.
You have broken the code,
Eaten of the fruit, transgressed
And made the snake your god.
World with end, world
At an end, you
Have touched the fiery fringes of
The throne of God!

And so the serpent has triumphed.
God gave you fire,
But you sought out his gift again
And were blinded by the light.

What footsteps will you leave
In sand or water? What
Fragile scent will remain on
The threshold of some other day?

This is a time for dragons and orphans.
The sea will not soothe you.
There is no still water.
Cain murders Abel,
And Abel murders Cain.

2.

      Zero is the hour,
Numbers turning back in space
To a point arbitrarily set by man,
Delving into time like a clock
Set backwards, not away,
Towards the hour
A slender pointer moves toward zero!

There is no sorrow.
Only numbers
And white clouds.

      One cloud like a turning wheel of sky
Grows upwards with the poignant
Beauty
Of a misty moon.
In the sunshine falls the toy,
Lost toy searching for its sunlight,
For its zero.
At the top, the flashing facets of great jewels appear,
Diamonds, rubies, amethysts, all shaped like tears.

3.

      Far beneath the pilot
Over geometric grays and greens,
A folded angel's wing takes flight,
Great white lily that enfolds the world,
Rapacious bird that soars to zero
In the far historic past of minutes,
In the fury and the fire of blood,
Stained dust and bent steel.

      This was the lilac and the hyacinth among carnations.
This was man's sunlight, the final consummation.
      From on high,
The buildings seem like gravestones,
Laned and lined and gray between
The parks, the river and the sea.

In the sunshine falls the toy,
Lost toy searching for its sunlight,
For it's zero once again,
Searching for the children
As they play at school,
Searching for the mothers as they
Play at keeping house,
Gone to fight the war,
Searching for the temples,
Searching through the smell of food,
Searching for the tempest and
The winds of zero.

       This mathematics tumbling from the sky
Fused stars and sand, cement and steel,
Newly dead with ancient dead,
Paolos and Francescas whirled
By fiery winds, lips transformed by terror
In a kiss forever incomplete.
Violet shadows rutted roads,
And the thousand haloes of the bursting sun
Trembled luminous, resplendent,
Above the growing solitude.

       There is no grief,
Only numbers.

4.

       The sky, the perfumed sky of August
Vaulting high above the ashen earth
Sees nothing.
Not the strange metallic bird,
Not the pilot,
Not the watch, ticking slowly.
There is a sound of motors
In the sky and in the sea.
The water is not still.
We walk in the valley of the shadow
Without rod or staff
To comfort us.

➤➤

JERRY HICKS

Newsmen Admit, Al-Jazeera Most Accurate News Coverage

Washington
London

blasted
Al-Jazeera

after
network

carried footage
from Iraqi television

of dead coalition
soldiers and

prisoners
of war,

repeated images
of Iraqi civilians

badly wounded
in air strikes . . .

Day 21, bomb
kills newscaster

destroys Al-Jazeera
news bureau.

Regrettable
states U.S. spokesperson.

➤➤

the first day of war

she shrouds herself in doubt
walks narrow lines between cracks
opens doors   quick closes
turns away like the cat
who sits   licks paw
after falling or when the bird got away
but nothing got away nothing was caught
she moves room to room gazing out each window
measuring bare ground
and snow cover late this year

she has breakfast in the diner about to close
diner and woman born the same year
it is too cold
all the news is bad
stone statues lichen grizzled in the cemetery
know more warmth than the passerby

she touches the pavement thinks
she feels rumble and blast
knows history is eaten for lunch
and forgotten

➤➤

Shelleen McQueen

Red, White and Blues

*After Marvin Gaye, The Four Tops, The Rolling
Stones, and my friend, Rick D.*

*Darlin', you're so great,
I can't wait for you to operate.*

End of Physics class
pack the car, haul ass.
Rick my love-friend,
soon swoon again.
Down the lake giggle talk
strong arm around me walk.
Beach blanket high,
life skulks, hides.

*Baby, I need your lovin',
got to have all our lovin'.*

Numbers fall fast, fade . . .
Broken boys in body bags
Sent home in hundreds every day.
Rick loses lottery, gets picked
Date of Entry draws near.
Hours disappear,
minutes into moment
our last breath together.

*Leaving just your picture behind
and I've kissed it a thousand times.*

C-130 transport takes him
Waikiki, then Nam.
Letters fast and fervent,
fat with photos,
without warning stop.
Rumor mill grinds slowly
through town to me.

I see a line of cars and they're all painted black
with flowers and my love both never to come back.

Brain bucket busted —
Closed casket.

➤➤

Neil English

Packing Crate

With an undertaker for a friend,
Dad always seemed comfortable with death;
helped Billy deliver bodies
whenever he needed an extra hand
(with the heavy ones)
or just rode along in the hearse
for conversation
on the long distance transport,
carting some anonymous out-of-stater
on his final trip home.

It came home to roost
in the summer of '67,
the long, olive drab packing crate
and Dad, with that depression-born
use-it-up make-it-do mentality,
filled it with shelves,
painted out the name stenciled on the side
missing somehow the letters "PFC."

He transformed that coffin case
to a peace-time use.
Against the cellar wall it stood,
as if at attention,
a dark, safe place
for Mother's canning —

stewed tomatoes, dill beans,
bread and butter pickles.

I could never approach the cupboard
without dwelling on the nameless "PFC."

When I returned from Vietnam
that April day in '72,
checked out the house from top to bottom,
in hopes nothing had changed in my absence,

the olive drab sarcophagus . . .
was gone.

→→

JUNE COLEMAN MAGRAB

Dear Jon

For Jon Grabowski, 1967–2001

An airplane crashes into The World Trade Center where you've been
working for only six days. 97th floor. We are told — *incinerated*. A friend
calls to wake me — *turn on the radio*. I get through to Erika and ask her
how she is. *It's not me, it's Jon.*

A memorial service, suicide attempts, rage, denial — grief's harder to
come by. Erika is still awash in memories, relives time with you where
these things don't happen. Innocence? No More. Sometimes I think my
daughter's a shell. A hard nut. Even a blood vessel about to burst. No
weekend is again like any other. No movies. No theater. No opera.

Three months after 9/11 Erika has a tree of life burned into her back with
your birth and death dates. One side all branches, the other two leaves
remaining, ready to fall. She knows from the moment it hits the news. No
hope. Ever. Then, without warning on March 11th 2002 a knock comes at
the door. 7:30 a.m. *Police! Come to the morgue. They've identified him.*

Four and a half inches of your pelvis. We pick you up six weeks later from a mortuary. A length of cigar divided between Erika and your mother. I sit there with you in a paper bag next to me telling you how much I miss you. Tell you no one should ever have to go through this. You in two tiny urns, each in a box both in a paper bag.

➳

JUNE COLEMAN MAGRAB

Hotel Chelsea Savoy

For Jon Grabowski 1967–2001

Wake Up. Wake Up. You Have a Daughter in New York
and a Husband in Washington

1.
A cabin in the woods, no television, just a radio
Describing four winged bullets loaded with passengers.

2.
The sky is bleeding.
The world has turned to ash.

3.
I'm holed up in one room or another in and out
of reality waiting for my daughter to kill herself.
Her husband incinerated three years ago, no grieving.
There are two to save, maybe more — my daughter's sister,
fragile as a humming bird, cares for her. Black widow.

Fruit flies swarm over ripened flowers, nuts grow stale
in the indigo vase, apricots turn into old men.
The widow guesses what he'd look like; his father's bald
thick around the middle, someone's donated kidney inside,
calloused knees, so much for god.

He had a name but all I see is blonde. At twenty-two loopy curls,
defiantly longer each year until his thick bob was drawn into a ponytail.

Gilded boy/man so beautiful
he sang with the angels,
looked at my daughter whenever his eyes were open.
In the name of god for the promise of eternity
he was murdered because he was
on time for work.

4.
I have no metaphors or similes, no fancy poetry.
I go from one room to another
in a strange city.

\>-

MICHAEL MACKLIN

Toll Call

In the dark   in nightmare   I woke naked
holding the phone
standing twenty feet from my bed
a voice said, "Terry died tonight
under the full moon by the Mekong River."

Perhaps he had been remembering Michigan when the mortar hit
a place he had touched and smelled and carried daily
a bit of earth molding in a folded Camel wrapper
kept in his pocket against the distance

Most of my life, wars have raged
at a distance   over there   across the room
fleeting visions of choppers and body parts
the blooming flame in someone else's night.

Rarely a threat to the safety of my room, this house, my family
bloodless and comfortable at the horizon of newscaster's lips
while I sat in this fishbowl, deaf and untouched
worrying about the important things:

School work   groceries   my lover's birthday
I could start and stop the dying with a remote
for Christ's sake no blood on my carpet
able to hold my future son with my two good arms.

I refused to go to Nam   so sensible
the right thing for me   the only way   I knew
to slow the bleeding
put out the flames . . .

But friends went and the sons of strangers
the daughter of the man beside me on the subway
Shari's boyfriend, Terry, the quiet guy
from the back row of chemistry.

Perhaps he had been remembering Michigan when the mortar hit
the long whine in my ear could have been the dial tone
of disconnect or the whistle of an incoming round
It has never left me   that silence
the crazed screaming of shells   the emptiness of a heart
no longer beating.

→⤝

CJ Heck

Taps

A gentle breeze chatters the leaves
as birds sing their greetings.
The sun shines on a day like any other,
and yet like none before.

Two mirrored rows of uniforms
are lined like blue dominoes,
their white gloves holding rifles at the ready.

One lone bugle cries out of its sorrow.
Twenty-four notes,
each note, slow as a tear,
blankets ears and heavy hearts.

In the silence between,
even nature holds its breath.
Gone is the wind.
Gone are the bird songs.
Gone the last hold on composure,
all lost in the bugle's lament.

Solemnly, a soldier approaches
and white gloves present a tri-fold flag.

And in one final, mournful note,
legions of silent voices unite
to call a comrade home
and a young wife weeps.

→►

NANCY DONOVAN

The Bagpiper

A lone piper stood upon the beach.
Ramrod straight, he held his pipes
And gazed beyond the sea.

Amazing Grace
Reached across the waves,
Proud and mournful tones
As once were called
Across glens and hills
Of Scottish Highlands

Taps followed.
The beach beside the sea
Felt holier than a church.

Coming to attention
In his Marine dress Blues
The young piper saluted
And walked away.

It would have been sacrilege
To question the moment.

→►

WILLIAM HEYEN

The Dead

I prayed through Graveyard Zero
deep as prayer can get
birds screaming in my ear
I thought I'd brained my head

cranes trucks dozers un-
layering cursive steel
each of a hundred stories
crushed to a foot of rubble

to grief's passionate rote
to mute omniscient heaven's
slashes of beak & wing
into windows & spinal columns

into our day's confused
carcinogen of thought & flame
the dead transformed to birds
can we hear them

doves moan our pavement
kestrels grind bones
ducks hiss radium water
thunderbird keens

sightings of the flying ones
double-helixed in toxic dust
bankrupt codes
in formaldehyde spirit

Buddhist Jew Christian Muslim
believers in peace
last human millennium
prepare your voice

✈

DAVID CONNOLLY

To the Vietnamese Veterans

I've wanted to tell you all,
as I've met each of you over the years;
"Tôi mang dâú dau thúóng cho Vietnam."
I bear the mark of pain for Vietnam.

No matter which side you were on,
know the war has cost me and is long over for me.
I hope it is over for you,
especially if it was between us.

But is what I have said the truth?
For what do I bear that mark?
Did I almost fall for your homeland
or for mine?

Was it that challenge to "Ask not,"
and Kennedy's Camelot?
Was it for me, my father, or yours,
for Southie, the States, or Saigon?

See, all of you,
on both sides,
can know and say for what it was you dared,
maybe almost died.

And all of you,
can say you fought for,
bear the mark of pain for,
your country, for Vietnam.

I fought for something,
something I cannot yet name.
that is the truth,
and the problem.

SAMUEL HAZO

Unspoken

The day the troops marched back
from desert bivouacs in Iraq,
their families knew their war would still go on.
Some never said a word
of what they saw and heard
while some thought long on what they'd undergone

like men remembering a year
of shock and awe and fear
created and imbedded by official lies.
For what they had to do
some lost their limbs, others
their testicles, and some both eyes.

A few were willing to go back
and join the next attack
because they missed their brothers in the war.
The rest resumed their lives
with families or wives
but never were the men they were before.

No matter where they went
they heard the President
give praise and credit for the price they paid.
But that said nothing new
since that's what leaders do
to blur the reasons for the wars they've made.

Though nothing can be said
to resurrect the dead,
we search for words that tell us what they gave
while cemeteries we create
with due allegiance to the state
speak differently in silence, grave by grave.

➻

ROBERT J. DUFFY

Heroes' Welcome

Regard
the faces of your children
coming so hard back,
their eyes the mad
magnesium white
of artificial stars.
On sleeve and shoulder
clawed like scars they wear
the shameful marks of learning.
Point and flank they patrol
your city's rubbled mansions
battered pavements,
kicking fragment glass
finger-searching darkness
for your tunnels, traps, trips
and mines.

Heed
you cry. Have we not
for you fashioned
just such careful laws to keep?
Come, be home again
and sleep as safe as
crocodile babies
in their Nile father's jaws.
But they, not heeding,
only stand and listen
over Jordan for the oiled
chant of engines
coming to lift them out.
Or seek blue veins
with needle sharpened
nipples and the clear
sweet milk of nodding
. . . nodding.

Tell us,
what do such ruined lions
dream behind their bars;
that liquid posture,
yellow eye, the clench
and quake of a muscle
shedding a fly. Of hunting
wild again across a vast
unstopping plain that raises
dust on every twist of air
into a dry resemblance
of prey, a husk of their
beloved enemies?
Or of meadows fresh prepared
for yet another wintery
scattering of red and flesh
like seed that, this time,
surely, must be springtime
resurrected innocent
and green?

Listen
to their damaged music
comes from every wheel
and hammer beaten round
with drums. They gather
at their barrel fires
and shake down
sounding wonders
from their hair,
chant the old-time
angry hymns they cannot
anymore believe. A rage
and melancholy choir,
they warm their half-gloved
fingers and shuffle
cobble-broken boots
and stare.

Pass them
corner-eyed and gone
in your doorways huddled
under bridges only glimpsed
and lost, seen through
shaded glass, a scrap of coat,
a cheek, a hand, a steam
of breath. Do they speak?
But what can they tell?
They goad with sticks
the entrails of the carrion
you leave beside your road
and prophesy
some great day of
happy returns,
some Saturday night
of laughter and dance
and brilliantine
and worms.

-►-

Cyclorama

A Navy man, a Nam and Storm vet, I'm long retired and newly wed. My wife and I visit Gettysburg. Through the slow beat of windshield wipers we peer out at the Virginia Monument, the North Carolina, Georgia, Arkansas, Texas, Alabama monuments. We look down on the Bushman Farm, the Slyder Farm.

> jungle coast
> a friendly-fire missile
> melts our main mast

We decide not to hike up, through the rain, to Big Round Top, but seeing the short distance to Little Round Top, we stop and go up. I read the plaques, circle the monument, look at the statues. I gaze down on Devil's Den.

> burning fields
> mask odors of desert heat
> carrier flight deck

We pass the Pennsylvania Monument, the Vermont Brigade. I get out and walk to the high Water Mark and stare out over the vast fields. This misty rain reminds me of cannon smoke. The Union soldiers, busy stopping Pickett's men, would have seen. I cannot bring myself to step onto such blood soaked ground. My wife takes my hand.

> Cyclorama
> "the next show starts in ten minutes
> come see the battle"

I'm having trouble telling where the rain ends.

->-

Reunion at the Vietnam Women's Memorial Dedication

She leans into my body.
Hotdance enters my stiletto heels.
"Teri, is that you?" she asks.

Her eyes insist I must remember how to
    bandage raging arms
    stitch emptied eye sockets
    dam up blood rivers
    wipe the spit.

She waves her thin arms into the night.
Timedance slows me in its coopered circle.
"Teri, is that you?" she demands.

Her hands steady me as I
    lift the jackknifed torso
    shift the limp penis
    soak up the soup of urine
    stroke the crusting skin.

She breathes her words into me.
Slowdance spears me to the hardwood boards.
"Teri, is that you?" she whispers.

Her voice requires me to
    hum the fucking Beach Boys
    lie in the knuckles of that one thin sheet
    reread Siddhartha
    accept the sweat of her hand.

Nodance slithers down my aching spine.

➤➤

PAUL NICHOLS

In the Clutches of the Beast

                              Prowling, seething
                              fangs and talons bared

The silent marauder lunges

                              Like a dull jackknife across knuckles

when that one trusted cog

                                        fails

when that one solid keeper

                                        abandons

when basic faith

                                        vaporizes

The cloaked deception mangles

                              Like a dildo lashed to a pervert

intruding
emerging
unrelenting violation

                              Bend over — touch toes
                         Stand straight — evoke attention
                              Sit and relax for a spell
                         Attempt a daydream — try sleeping

The rape is perpetual

                         Vintage scars streak the surface
                            veiled as bygone pain
                         Raised, sunken, bridging holes
                              none is superficial

                         Parasitic demons lurk fathoms deep
                            Name them, the shaman says
                         Occupying forces, latent impostors
                              eluding nomenclature

Unleashed, the predator stirs

> Creeping malignance
> surging hunger
> familiar quarry

The Beast pulsates to be nourished

➤

JACK HALEY

I Fell in Love with a Woman of the Opposite Sex

You were brought to my attention by another
this place I am brought calls me, you wouldn't
let go of my senses, Circe is Greek for hawk,
branches don't fly while the hawk waits
trapped in the tenth book where the dead run wild
I'm pronounced dead one by one, my heart is
as black as the silk pajama armor I once pierced
feasting on my bullets they lay down content
where are all the bullets buried in all the bodies
buried in the ground?
I'm the prodigal son with no father
white lesbian women nurture me
while doing an autopsy they found traces of Con Thien
in my system, a search of the battlefield produced
the following revisions that only the dead could know
the meaning of, secretly I want to eat her necklace.
Thank You,
Jack.

➤

BILL DOLLOFF

The Bloody Bed They Made

Bring along your M16 and carry our brother too.
Keep your head down low, my friend, and I will cover you.
Bullets flying and bombs in the air
Sing with me brothers under the glare.

Doc's on his way, brother, you hold on.
I'm not in the mood to tell them you're gone.
Don't erase him from the roster, sir, he's still alive.
If doc gets here soon, he may make it home.

Bandages and tourniquets don't make a damn!
They went to tell the Colonel he's lost another man.
I brought along my M16, I brought my brother too.
Keep your head down low, my friend, and God will cover you.

They buried him with honors at the end of his life.
I kept his medals and his badges and even his knife.
Doc came to see me, said that I'm fine, but
I should let him know if these dreams come back.

O' say can you see by the dawn's early light?
Today is just another day followed by a night.
The Germans, the Japanese, the Viet Cong,
They're all in your mind, son, they're long since gone.

My family hasn't seen me for nearly six years.
I can't cry anymore, I'm all out of tears.
My gun is rusty, my bullets gone, they took them away
But I search and hope to find them each and every day.

My brother asks me, do you have my badges and my knife?
I'll keep you safe in my soul, try to save your life.
The nurse is coming soon, but don't be afraid.
I'll be lying next to you in the bloody bed they made.

➻

KATE LEIGH

Angel of Grace

We find you
On the side streets of Brooklyn
Or in a high school
Cafeteria, leftover
Of the human race.

Your bare arms,
The lace
Of stretched
And shattered flesh,
Your face the guise
Of guilt met innocence,

On mounds of bones
Left waste upon the fields
Of Nam, Afghanistan, Iraq,

A trace of some uncurdled
Blessing of the human race.

➤➤

JOHN-MICHAEL ALBERT

Apple Blossoms, Splinters and Flames

For my father, Wilmer E Albert

Is it really possible for daddy's favorite to lose his way in the world?

From his vantage in the white church steeple, he trained
his binoculars on the distant mountain and radioed
reports to Command on the long files of German troops
entering a tunnel in the French Alps. After a productive

Can a young Latin scholar and church organist walk away from both?

morning in darkness and heat, breathing musty air, standing
in bird and bat shit; and weighed by unrelenting loneliness and fear,
he climbed down from his aerie and sat against a tree
under an April shower of white and pink apple blossoms.

What, in this photograph of a handsome US Army Sergeant on leave

He gnawed and ground his foraged meal (thick smoked ham,
and sharp cheese on coarse, grainy bread), wondering
what his brothers were up to, three in Europe, one in Asia.
The steeple suddenly exploded into splinters and flames;

in Paris, belies the alcohol and violence lurking in his future?

the iron bell tumbled from the sky and shattered on a gravestone
three paces from his road-worn soles, four from his loaded pistol.

➤➤

ALDO TAMBELLINI

mother

mother
it is the night
they come
with the white van
three strangers
dressed in white
&
I as a decoy
have tricked you
into descending the stairs
in the january snow
falling
with the whitest of white
the white van
with the backdoor opened
parked by

66

that ancient poplar tree
on james street
in syracuse ny
the three men in white
acting
as a matter of fact
used to a routine
that must be performed
best in a swift way
you mother
suddenly aware of
what is about to happen
hold on to my arm
pleading
don't
let them take me away
you are my son
don't do it
they ease you
with assured moves
inside the white van
it all happens
so quickly
the door closes
pulls away
from the spot
under the street lamp
next to the ancient poplar tree
then
I walk around
continuously
till the footprints wear out
the fresh snow
to the deeper layers
of frozen ice
the white snow falling
in the white night
of my under seventeen years of life

the footprints deeper
than the roots sinking
god knows
to what depth under the street
near the dark
wood ornate house
from another century
where we rented the darkness
of an apartment
there within months
the madness descended
you desperately
trying to have me enter
the reality
of your tortured visions
wanting to share
the suspicion of everything
pointing to devices
hidden in various places
under floors
behind walls
in ceiling lights
whispering
so no one would hear
cautioning every move
as to protect me
from invisible forces
the endless times
I searched
showing you
there was nothing there
but it was all
so real to you
the war
the foreign country
in the very city
where in another time

you gave birth to me
they took you away
in the whitest night
to the state hospital
in upstate ny

->-

PATRICIA FRISELLA

Prayer for My Father

Like the red-faced glassblower fusing and slumping in *mondo fiamma*,
my brain is on fire. Conflicted memories of my hero, my enemy,
like a thermal shock, make my glass eye crackle to life.
I'm looking for the good in all this, but it's hot as hell.
Flat as a puddle, I crawl away from the clowns

and long nights of dreaded howling, flickering illumination,
search lights, and police cars. There are no pistol locks,
gun safes, classes to save me. Each day I come back
like the ringed cormorant that dives for fish it cannot swallow,
slave to the man who feeds it.

I remember the flames of a home burning down, the snap
of dry wood, the explosion of windows. I remember the heat
of hungry mouths yawning open and black and smelling of soot.
I remember the hands, hot as pistons, that burned
what they touched. I remember my life turning to ash.

After ritual roastings at the asylum, he wonders about feeling
tree or stone to confirm his life. I say what's to be lost
by contact. Like the woman in Aarhus struck by lightning
who flickered for years between life and death in a coma
then woke up craving Greenland, I am hungry.

I want to go to that land of long winters where heaven cracks
and burns. I want to go to Siberia where I can hear the crystal beads
of my breath tinkle frozen to the ground. Time nibbles my obelisks,

gnaws my smokestacks. No one smears his face with dirt and tears
like Achilles at the loss of a friend or a father unafraid of his own blood.

When I come back from the abundant zone
of polar ice, of dreary dawns, I promise
to rid you of your fiery touch and your dark moods
to fill your mouth with the glass harmonium's music.

→→

DAVID PELOQUIN

Eulogy

I.

I see you at the supper table
surrounded by your family,
keeping us at bay
with your newspaper wall
and your voice
rolling and rumbling guttural thunder —
your political tirades
brewing a storm,
your outbursts finally
exploding like gunfire
over our heads,
a barrage of fire and smoke;
hot spent brass casings
littering the kitchen floor
at our feet.
And smoke.
Always more smoke.

Smoke fills the rooms of memory
and will not blow away.
Even when I open all the windows
and all the doors.
Even when I smash the windows

and tear the doors
off their hinges.
The shells are long gone,
swept up and stored
in dark olive green canvas sacks
hidden deep in our bones.
But the smoke
from all that fire
has never cleared.

2.

The ground you stood on
was indeed solid,
but it was not fertile ground.
No grass
no flowers
no fruit bearing trees
grew in that barren soil,
and little of the garden
I have grown in my own life
has been planted from any cutting
nurtured in your patch of weeds

And yet —
I forgive you.
Even now as I drag from my gut
this smell of burnt flesh.
Even now as I haul from the basement of my childhood
decades of rank, yellowed newspapers
and countless empty beer bottles
filled only with the lost years
of your life,
I forgive you
even now as I pull
from my bone marrow
these ash-gray lines —
each verse a heavy olive green sack.
Each word a cold, tarnished brass shell.

3.
Three years at war
and upon your return,
no hatred for
German or Japanese —
only an endless
railing rant
against those
who send other men's sons
to fight their sordid battles
of greed and power.

You,
my father,
with no father of your own,
knew little of how a man
expresses his heart.
That part of you was kept locked
and unborn behind your cynical anger,
your tireless criticism,
and we,
your sons and daughters
and your wife,
suffered for that.

Wounded at birth,
no father to follow
into your own manhood,
we forgave you
and loved you
as best we could.

✈

RODGER MARTIN

Toes

"Lonely toes, I have lonely toes,"
His daughter ployed as she stretched
on the backseat then propped her feet
between the Chevy's front seats.

In that tired Sunday evening drive
he took one toe market, one toe home,
and she relaxed with a moon smile
that filled him with wonder and rage
because his love's a bone stump hacked by a dull axe.

She wiggled and he squeezed past
the staccato chop of bullet and blade
that stacked boys into medevacs,
their splintered knees gristly white
protrusions through the strands
of ligament and tendon that once hooked them
to calves and shins still laced into boots
left crazy quilt on the ground.

She squiggled and he clawed further back
to the burning oil of a mother,
doped with morphine, missing her breasts,
half her weight, her tallowed head dropping
clumps of black hair in the best radioactive style.
Still she could smile recognition to her child
while filthy surgical hands pushed him,
pushed him out of her room.

He screamed into the present,
clung to a daughter's toes
as if they could stomp,
as if they could kick
and boot him, boot him, boot him
out of his past.

➤

ELLEN HERSH

War Games

Every day after school
snipers hide behind the brown November bushes,
dart and duck and fall upon the ground.
Crisp air echoes dull reports of rifles,
ack-ack of machine guns.

Heavy mist and falling dusk;
lights come on in windows,
lanterns in the forest of the Ardennes,
behind brown shades in London,
in castles up and down the Rhine.

Nacht und Nebel on Main Street:
little boys playing guns,
Desert Storm,
while moms behind the windows
sew on Cub Scout patches:
Den 4, Pack 29,
Fourth Armored, Eleventh Airborne.
Mothers sitting sewing,
sweetly sewing,
gold star mothers
with candles in their windows?

Kid warriors laugh and say good-bye,
dispersing fast for supper.
Nights I notice in the dark of early winter,
once the streets are bare,
beams from cars on Main Street,
passing the town hall,
light up the Honor Roll
beneath the empty flagpole
war dead etched in stone.

→►

MARGARET BRITTON VAUGHN

Maneuvers

About two hundred feet
from the mailbox
that sat across the dirt road
from my uncle and aunt's house
grew a thicket,
where camouflaged uniforms
tried to blend with nature.
From the front porch
we strained our necks
and watched FDR's soldiers
divide into our side
and Germany's side.
Our swing's noisy, rusty chain
creaked with each shot,
and we flinched
while rockers stopped
in a forward position.
They left behind brass
shells that some
people made lamps of.
With the exception
of Uncle Will's picture
in his uniform
that sat on the mantel,
this was as close as we
got to the war.

➼

Hilary Holladay

Summer of Love

"Sometimes I dream of at last becoming a child."
— Robert Duncan

Wearing a homemade white dress with red cherries on it,
she runs across dry grass crackling under midday sun,

then holds up her kindergarten diploma
and smiles into a world where maples surround the old stucco house

and her parents and sisters are always around,
their laughter coming from one room or another.

That night, when stars pierce the darkness
and slip inside her summertime dreams,

sorrow passes beyond her brow, lets her rest.
This will always be a happy day.

She stirs within me

Forever after, she can have Vietnam and Blackness,
the potent power of flowers.

She can research riots and read up on rebellion.
She can attend seminars, then teach them, teach them all.

For now, she has hung up her new dress,
and the colorful diploma uncurls in moonlight.

Far away, college freshmen are taking LSD for fun,
soldiers are swearing in the Laotian rain.

Some of the dying live on.
What is the legacy they leave her?

The telling of time, an alphabet there for the asking.

➤➤

STEPHEN WING

Somewhere Children Do Not Play at War

You can't blame me for flinching
back against the wall
when a small boy points his
pistol at me and yells, "Pow! Pow! Pow!"

I am lying back there somewhere
feeling the sidewalk as if I'd never touched
sunshine, pumping out my urgent
puddle

And when three kids dash by, invisible
in their camouflage sneakers,
chattering on their walkie talkies,
pay no attention if I button my opinion
and pocket my fingerprints

I crouch somewhere in a black, sweaty
silence too small for me,
listening to voices muffled by cinderblocks
or years

And when I wake this morning
to jubilant cries, and look out to see twins
in miniature green berets waiting
while a man in uniform unlocks the station wagon,
forgive me if I drop the curtain and start
smuggling my unborn children across the border

Somewhere I am waiting for my daughter
to come home, holding grief in
as one who holds a breath too long
under water

➤

CYNTHIA HUNTINGTON

The Invasion of Canada

Close to the border of my native land
a soldier goes up into the mountains,
pressing a boundary no one has seen.
He is carrying a gun, and a radio
whose antenna scrapes the air like a
beetle's feet. The soldier hopes
to hear Mozart. He gets baseball.
Another station has news: the world will end
in fire in thirteen weeks. Prepare.
He turns off the radio and the dead begin
singing to him. "Come home. Come home."
Their voices beguile him — but what do they mean?
Where is his home: this wilderness
or the other just beyond? Perhaps
he has already crossed over and is wandering
into that final country that will claim him forever.
In the mountains, among pines, beside a small stream
that runs left and right over rocks,
fast and shallow and loud, he sits and weeps.
His destiny is too big.
No one invades a nation anymore.
Not alone, on foot, with a gun and a radio.
His loneliness is cold water
that makes the rocks shine. Great stillness
where he is. Then, slowly, birds.

➤➤

CLEOPATRA MATHIS

Mother's Day, 1993:
Hearing We Will Bomb Bosnia

You so love the child, you take away
every unsafe thing, surround him
with softness as he sleeps. You have no way,
truly, to keep him unharmed, and knowing this,
you live with a certain condition, a swelling
in the complicated region of the chest.
It catches you unaware this lovely morning
as you drink your second cup of coffee,
twenty minutes past his usual waking. You resist
what-if, reminding yourself
he hardly slept last night. You've learned
what asthma can do; you've seen his blue face
when the airways close, then for days, dull
shadows under his eyes. Called from sleep,
you've found him sitting up, both hands braced
against the wall. You hold him
tight in your arms, his thin shoulders, trunk, hips
racked with coughing, every muscle and nerve
negotiating the art of breathing. And though
you've bought the machine that like magic
opens his tubes and restores the air, sweet gulps
he takes in like a drug, and gives him back to perfect sleep,
every bizarre consequence you've ever heard
comes rushing through like a wind in spring,
a sharp risk in the blossoming world.

No wonder you turn, horrified and hating
your cowardice, from the magazine, the cover picture
of the dead child. You can't look at it:
the shrouded head, the bloody mouth
exposed and slack, then the brief, unchildlike clothing
and below that, exposed,
as if nothing in the world were wrong,

the tender arc of the belly.
Oh that familiar part of the child, the body
a mother kisses. A nation of mothers.

➤

CURT CURTIN

Item

Based on a 2004 story by a British reporter in the Congo

He holds his mother, or somebody's mother
with wasted arms. How does he choose
among the mothers, all bony and gray
heaped in an open grave? *He only said*
she looked as if she could be his.

The reporter chokes at the sight, an open sore
that he cannot read as merely another item:
"Child Grieves in the Heart of Africa."
He takes the boy from the numberless flies
and death in heaps, a scene that could fill
an inside page, and brings him to a hospital.

Next day when the reporter returns, hope in hand,
chocolate — that's what brings relief, ask any child
on your street, *Oh no*, they say, *that boy has died.*
But why? *He decided not to live any more,*
and so he died.

And so.
Too dry for tears, too dumb with grief, he chose;
and all the mothers, and all the others in the grave
drew the inconsolable child to their embrace.

Where are the arms that made that grave?
They are cradled in secret understanding,
wrapped in blood soaked flags,
nursed on the pap of lies and apathy.

Drawn by deadlines' press on a day like others
when so many strive for fame or die, we tire,
but do not decide to die. What is enough —
hugging his mother or one that could be —
enough to open a column with aid.

→>

JERRY HICKS

Issues of War

The 1970's

Aqua marine lapping
the black rocky shore
bordering the Corniche
the loudest sound —
a prelude.

Beirut celebrates Sabbath
Friday, Saturday, or Sunday
just as Paris or Los Angeles,
but streetcars no longer ply
bomb contorted Rue Bliss.

Today, the Christian Sabbath,
Israeli piloted F-16's
shatter the calm of a sleeping child's
nursery.
Bellowing clamor of explosions.

AUB, my alma mater,
flounders in Ras Beirut —
a torpedoed carrier
unable to launch; unable to sink.

Nearby children huddle.
Toy guns cleverly silenced,

boys shout in whispers
dash about on soft, frightened feet —
pretending childhood
has meaning — if not color.

Once, wistful-eyed Phoenician women
fed pyres pine and incense
to light mariners home;
now descendants numbly,
in gasoline, burn dead children.

→-

LEE NEWTON

Why We Make Love

It's a Baby Boom, of sorts,
this generation, the 200 born
in one month at Fort Campbell,
the 350 conceived at Fort Bragg
when their mothers and fathers
returned from deployment.

I include my twin sons
born nine months after September 11
when I look at them and know, sadly,
they weren't planned, not even
the faintest of considerations.

Maybe those are the best lives —
those who fall into this world
unexpectedly, some beautiful
perennial, unannounced and staking
its claim in the Spring garden—maybe.

Because of me and people like me,
I worry, still, question what will occur
decades from now. Wonder what happens

one morning when they sit at their tables,
ankles crossed, flipping through the *Post*
or *Times*, their fingers painted, stained
with speculative theory, academic conjecture.

What will become of us when they learn
they were not created out of love, lust,
even infatuation, when they discover
so many of us fell into arms and cold beds
out of some primal, instinctual necessity?
What, when they determine they are merely
a product of our sorrow, guilt, and fear?

Maybe it is then we will find ourselves
in a revolution—this angry generation
forcing us to confront our inabilities
to cope, to handle life. Or maybe
they will just stop, stop on the porches,
decks, stand there—newspapers rolled
and under arms—finally understanding
the frailty of our species, the clutter
and confusion of their own lives.

➤➤

LAURE-ANNE BOSSELAAR

Leek Street

      In Bruges, was a cul-de-sac so narrow
cars never scarred its mossy cobblestones.
Every house had a niche above the door
for a Saint, and a little garden framed by high
brick walls. Carved into the back rampart,
an iron gate opened on the Wool Canal.
      Now and then, a muskrat's head
pearled out of that green velvet, then slipped
back into the water. The Belfry rang a bronze
quiver through the drizzle every quarter.

83

Yochemke lived at No. 8 in the only house
with open curtains and no Saint.
He was nine, had a large hole in his tongue
and six numbers tattooed on his arm.
They did this to him when he was a baby, he said,
he couldn't remember if it hurt.
I loved him so much I repeated the numbers
inside his arm every night until I fell asleep:
Yochemke-seven-four-three-two-three-six
        It rained the day he said I could put
my finger through his tongue.
He shut his pale gray eyes, I shut mine,
and he slowly closed his lips around my finger.
Something guilty and deep made me want to cry.

        We were setting muskrat traps by the canal
the first time he said he loved me. I wanted
to play the piano for him, or have curly hair
and be beautiful, I was so happy.
        The muskrats were for his father
who made collars and muffs out of them
to sell at the Fish Market. He always came
back with something for Yochemke. Once,
it was a glass marble with a heart of green,
blue and gold. When Yochemke gave it to me,
we were sitting by the canal stirring the algae
with willow sticks. His father had told him
the heart of the marble was what the world
looked like before the Germans.

        That night, we climbed the Belfry tower
to make the bronze bell ring with the marble.
Up there, looking down at the brown roofs
and fields of the world, we wanted to change it back
to how it was, make it look like the marble again.
        We'd set traps for the Germans, poke
holes in their tongues, hurl their bodies in the canal,
and all the muskrats of Bruges would feed on them,
fatten, we'd trap them, and—

I'll buy you a piano, said Yochemke,
  we'll be the richest muff makers in Belgium.

Then, with our marble, we tapped the bell
as hard as we could and listened to its small sound
float out over the canals.

→-

CLEOPATRA MATHIS

Cleopatra Theodos

We had language between us: her trick
of pretending not to know English
when she didn't want to speak. I pretended
not to know Greek, and so it went
that way for years, a clear stand off
in which she learned to get what she wanted
by staring deep into my face; the easy
track of my childhood never lied.
Her reward was my affliction: sties
flowered in my eyes. Around the iris
red flamed its way, evil she could see
settling in the rim. She knew some magic words,
province of one firstborn protecting another,
and she gave them, chanting and gesturing,
her face transfixed by mine.
Whatever the devil is, he listened
to her voice. She lured him out
into her atmosphere and pinned him to the meanest year:
to the twenty four hours her first child lived
and the scimitar's blade in her mother's belly,
its few minutes of wrath against hidden children.
Five brothers in a nation of murdered children
came back and spoke, safe for once
in the sanctuary of her face. Held there in Ayvali,
stone's throw from the ancient cities of grief,

the devil met his history. His gift for division
could not stand up to the power of her losses—
though he would keep coming back with his attempts
to burrow in, to follow the light
through the optic nerve leading to the back of the brain,
to that tiny center where the soul is housed.
But no matter how he tried
to fix the fine point of his greed,
she lifted my chin and studied his possibilities:
the little tear ducts beginning to swell,
some threat of cloud in the innocent blue.
Over me, she spoke for heaven. Words opened
her hands and bound me to her.
With that music, with the light of her eyes,
she whipped him, dismissed him, and he fled.

➼

CURT CURTIN

Kwan Yin's Eyes

In sleep I see a bird with Kwan Yin's eyes
calm as long sorrowing. It utters no song.
That bird in flight flutters like a windblown leaf.
She means the world is stirred by thoughtless winds
that strip the trees and blow the nests away.

The bird is seeking sympathy in the lives
of troubled ones. I only know they are
the Other. We listen together to dry wind
droning on unfretted strings. The tanbur hangs
on a jagged wall, fragment of an empty home.

An old man and a child have walked away
with lost desire for strings, six days on broken roads
to a border where they are turned away.
Dry wind on strings, empty lamentation
for the soul of another undone home.

The bird with Kwan Yin's eyes flutters
in a wounded way. She means to say the world
is shattering like scenes on Chinese teacups
thrown against ancient walls, all the walls
where people write their border lines

in splintered tongues and shattered sight.
The bird with Kwan Yin's eyes alights
on the tanbur, her wings spread wide across
the silent strings. She means that loud
disharmonies of hate and war abide

in towns where tanbur, sitar and lute
were heard in the homes and schools. Only
the wind now learns their unheard monodies.
Where are the children's fingers
that could play? They are stroking the dead,

they are holding wicked toys, they fly away.
The bird with Kwan Yin's eyes huddles
her wings and closes her eyes. She means
it is a long time, a passage through human
designs unraveling. The savage weds the savant

where there is no ceremony, nothing
but forward motion in immense disharmony.
In time the wind will subside, leaving
belief hanging like dry leaves waiting for spring,
waiting for children's fingers to play again.

➤➤

SAMUEL HAZO

Iraq

"Every day I think of Iraq,"
The President said.
For emphasis
he said it twice, but what
or even how he thought
he never said.
For me, Iraq
is a Marine sergeant, his right
sleeve empty from shoulder
to cuff, his right leg
fitted from the knee-stump
down with a black titanium
prosthesis levered to a fake
foot inside an Adidas shoe.
He walks like a man on a wire,
balancing, balancing, shunning
assistance with a shrug or a tight
smile.
That's his Iraq.
Mine is that flat, right sleeve,
that flexing brace, that shoe.

MICKEY CESAR

the charge

You know nothing of being alone,
she says, flashing storm, then sun,
lightning, rain.

He has an unshakable faith
that no sin exists
which nights of nakedness

cannot erase—
from the kitchen,
a faucet drips,
restaurant sounds drift
through the echo chamber:
silverware
chatter
dishes

you've never calculated
the kinetic energy of a threat
or the potential charge
in falling apart.

An unpainted door
turns back on its hinge,
releasing a sand-blown complaint
on the prairie, where he stands
all too aware
that no mountains are to be moved,
and there is no sea to be seen;
no river to drown in.

He's been reading poems
to Kelli by lamplight,
drawing in the margins
of cheap hotel Bibles
and supermarket scriptures;
she's been deconstructing blenders,
lamenting the inflexibility
of small instruments of torture,
and the utility of improvised explosive devices
for days, yet said nothing.

Nothing at all, she says,
you know nothing of being alone.

Church-bells ring in the distance.
Near nightfall, the neighbor
starts his lawnmower like always,
keeping a crooked eye on the Crocus.

➻

First Day, Container Corporation of America, June 1972

When the bleak break room smokers asked,
          "What you run?" I answered, "The half
and quarter mile," to which response

they burst in furious, gut-clutching
          yucks and howls. "No, boy," one said,
"What *machine* you run?" and I got it.

Both the joke I'd innocently made
          and the joke I was: high-school-Harry
among the balding, unionized sublime.

"Slitter 66," I said, and their blue
          ballooning guffaw burst in rarefied air,
everyone exhaling Lucky Strike at once.

Eighteen, big-haired and mutton-chopped,
          brand new black pocket tee taut over
my still tight gut, I thought they saw

the future in me and shuddered
          at their vision. Or was it their past,
themselves before the war to save

democracy—resplendent in white shirt
          and dungarees – now pot-bellied and shot?
The young think things like that.

How could I know the guy whose job I took
          came home boxed from Vietnam,
a war I fought in TV news clips

and the peace marches of us blessed
        with high draft numbers? I ate alone:
mother's cold meat loaf, bruised banana,

a Coke that gave me the jitters.
        When the horn burped, I lit out for work
like the apple polisher I'd planned to be,

though not before those men
        who'd seemed too gray had heaved me
in a tin bin of cardboard scrap

and slammed the lid, their fists beating
        rhythm to the heart thumping my throat.
Whatever republic we were then,

its pulse beat among us,
        though no one would say
the word. Sprawled head first

among mis-cuts and discards,
        the dross of a process I'd yet
to learn—man, this was a start.

                                —➤—

KEVIN STEIN

While I Burned the Autumn Garden

The fleck of ash that won't flick off, wounded
summer delivered into the arms of, well,
October. That's it, metaphor. A few clouds
in lank procession, fingering their white hankies,
and everywhere wind about to happen, poised
among the avuncular oaks like the friend
I'd trust to pick me up when my Ford's in shop,
friend who'd rescue me from the waiting room's

Field and Stream, Ammo News, the single, oily
kept-behind-the-counter Penthouse I once
witnessed a 16 year old sneak off to the john.
Rescue, think of that: a collusion of
happy gods amidst our pitiful collisions,
as years ago I wrapped a tourniquet
around the arm of a guy high on LSD,
his dutiful heart arcing blood right through
the window he'd shattered to teach giggling
sorority girls a visceral lesson in anti-war decorum.
The marchers were stoned. I had no choice:
the squad car, Emergency where doctors stitched
his architect's arm and cops took names.
I learned all things have their price,
first when gratitude looped my neck like a noose,
a rope yanked tight by each *thanks, man,*
then in court for malicious property damage.
Now this lustral swoon and collapse,
this late century age of Augustus, Horace growing old
amid the ceremony of ash and bitter wines.
All right, all right. I know Horace chastened Virgil,
"What we have no power to change,
we can learn to live with," an honorable man's lesson
in how to get by, get on. Try this then.
A singed pinch bug hauled another
through smoldering folds of pumpkin.
To hell with metaphor and its swayback horse:
While I burned the autumn garden,
Serb soldiers beat a man whose blood puddled
in Bosnian mud like blood puddling in mud.
I've no right to feel so powerless.

➵

DUDLEY LAUFMAN

Dioramas
are fascinating,
like the ones at Concord, Massachusetts,
depicting the battle at the bridge.
Or the three at Widner Library,
Harvard University, with details of Harvard Square
from the 1600s to the 1930s.

I made one to scale
of a dairy farm
on our ping-pong table.
The neighborhood boys didn't like it because
when they wanted to play gnip-gnop
they had to take it down and put it back
just the way I had it before.
They quit altogether when I got
real cowshit to enhance the scene.
I made another of Fenway Park
complete with the green monster
on my bedroom floor.

But I was blown away
when visiting Germany in 2005,
by the four in the Old Town Hall
in Hannover, Germany.
The first one is set in 1605,
a medieval city surrounded by a
star moat, farms and forest on the edge.
Next is 1939, a burgeoning city
complete with railroad, church steeples,
red roofs predominate in miniature detail
merging into the painted horizon.
Next one dated 1945,
the city is dull brown and gray ash.
Just gable ends and cellar holes, brick rubble.
The railroad station roof is full of holes.
Only the church and Town Hall remain.

We stood there heads bowed.
Even though we didn't do it,
we somehow felt responsible.

A man next to us said
Terrible isn't it.
He was short and balding,
smiling hesitantly.
Said, One good thing that came out of the war
was that we *kinder* could explore the ruins.
He said Every night the sirens would sound,
we would take a blanket and go to underground.

He told us his brother came home
with a bullet hole in one cheek and out the other.
They patched it up in hopes to
heal and stay home
but he was sent back to the front.
Never saw him again. Not a word.

He said Mother looked like Marlene Deitritch.
Father was killed
at the Battle of the Bulge.
In two years Mother
had aged to being
stooped and gray.
He held his clenched
hands beside his head
squeezed his eyes shut
saying I hate war
I chust hate war.

✈

PAT PARNELL

"Shock and Awe"

Exactly
my feeling
as I watched
the Twin Towers
crumple.

➤

BARBARA HOMANS

After the Bombardment

The tank rode over the garden,
bloodied the roses.
How angry the garden grew,
buds thrown everywhere like scattered tears.
Gone all possibility of daffodils next spring.
Fear is never alone.
The lilies clutched each other,
and the softened earth,
bent deep within itself,
sought shelter.

➤

BARBARA HOMANS

Thanksgiving

Deer hang from the trees.
Black ice lies on the road.
They have harvested the turkeys,
except for the President's reprieve.

And we sit before the television
to count the dead overseas.

In silence,
one by one,
their faces appear,
stay their few seconds,
then leave.

→-

Yamilé Craven

Aftermath

Medevac chopper descends—a black spider
against the red sky of the setting sun,

Its cargo—amputees, the maimed,
young men who will limp out their lives

In the year men are government pawns
on the chessboard of the gods of war—

And the sky over the planet
mirrors blood-red.

→-

Yamilé Craven

Who Listens

I sit alone in a room.
We are all alone in our thoughts.

The night spins emptiness.
I am cold under the orbit of stars.

When is the blood ever remembered?
Who can tell the pain?

The cat curls warm on the round pillow.
She remembers nothing.

What vibrates in the silence of space
From the planet's battlefields?

From the clashing fields of blood
Who listens?

In this quiet New England night of drifting snow
No one will hear the screams.

Like the curled leaves of the prayer plant
I prepare to sleep.

➤➤

THOMAS J. DIEGOLI

V2's

In the grainy black and white
    film clip I watched
    a young mother
    carefully dig
    the body of a small child
    from the rubble
    of their London home
    she held him close
    and rocked him and rocked him
    slowly in her arms
    I could not see her face
I held Peg tightly
    gratefully, crying silently
    and rocked her and rocked her
    slowly in my arms

The Hitlers
   Stalins
     Pol Pots
       the Saddam Husseins
       have rendered
       pacifism
       moot

→►

LESLEY KIMBALL

The Canvas of War, Vancouver Art Gallery

The paintings of war show dead and dying trees
standing sentinel over men, chaos and fire.
The wounding of the world should bring us to our knees.

We've come to see what such art achieves:
bare, tangled limbs pantomiming a funeral pyre.
The paintings of war show dead and dying trees.

Frame after frame, the air grows still with our unease;
dead landscapes cradle bodies, uniformed in the mire.
The wounding of the world should bring us to our knees.

To which gods can we appeal, what offer to appease
their vengeful spirits? Gods of war or art or higher?
The paintings of war show dead and dying trees.

Yes, soldiers too, dead and dying, who seize
our gaze and seem to cry through the haze as a choir:
The wounding of the world has brought us to our knees.

No patriotic speeches here: pain and paint frees
us from rhetoric, exposing the lie and the liar.
The paintings of war show dead and dying trees.
the wounding of the world will bring us to our knees.

→►

DON KIMBALL

On a Clear Day

You see
their ties,
like flags,
fly up
in furls
and you try
to close
your eyes

while they leap
or drop,
like wounded
birds
or rag-
dolls,
from fiery
towers.

How small
their bodies
seem
with all
that day-
light sprawling,
yet so
desperate
for what
will be
their last
calling . . .

➼

JOHN PERRAULT

Ashes to Ashes

After an AP photo of lower Manhattan, Sept. 11, 2001

Ash blankets the old graves
in Trinity Churchyard.

How hard it is for us to see
given the grain of the film,
given the smoke clouding the lens.

We stumble into the picture
squinting through dust,
holding our breath

straining to focus
on the stones
that have just this second
caught the camera's eye

gritty markers
sticking out of the rubble,
holding their ground
covered with loess.

We lean close
clutching the page
fixing our eyes
on each half-buried plot,
engraving each slab in our minds

even as the photographer
risks our lives

even as the temples
come crashing down around us.

➤➤

El Viejo Dictador

Stroessner está viejo
El despótico general está viejo.
Viejo como Pinochet. Viejo como Perón.
Viejo como Somoza,
Aunque a este, no lo dejaron envejecer.

Stroessner está viejo.
Viejo como su dictadura en mi memoria.
Esta mañana ví su foto en el diario.
Cumplió sus noventa.
El Viejo carnicero
Que hospedó a otros carniceros
Como él.
Ví su foto y me pregunté
Por todos los turturados y asesinados
Por su regimen. ¿Qué buscabas?
¿Qué fuerzas operaron en tu conciencia
Para que helado como el rayo
Talaras las vidas
De tantos rios que nunca llegaron al mar?
¿Que diabolicos designios compensaron tus desequilibrios
Para que construeras represas de silencio y muerte?
¿Que nefasto orden sostene tu negra arquitectura?
Y ahora estás viejo.
La muerte afila su guardaña y te espera.
Vos tendrás millonario entierro.
Y tu fortuna rapiñada entre coimas y armas
Se quedará aquí.

Cuando te estés deshaciendo en el cajón,
Tus pollos seguirán picoteando en el mismo gallinero.
Algunos quizás recuerden tus cacareos.
Pero las palabras de Roa Bastos
Y de muchos de tu pueblo,
Transcenderán las represas y seran agua
Para el mar y para el cielo.

GABRIEL FABIAN BAUTISTA

The Old Dictator

TRANSLATED BY CICELY BUCKLEY

Stroessner is old.
The despotic general is old.
Old like Pinochet.
Old like Perón.
Old like Somoza,
But they didn't let that one get old.
Stroessner is old.
As old as his dictatorship in my memory.
This morning I saw his photo in the news.
He has turned ninety.
The old butcher
Who harbored other butchers
Like himself.
I saw his photo and wondered
About all the tortured and assassinated
By his regime. What were you looking for?
What forces worked in your conscience
So that cold as lightning
You might cut short the lives
Of so many rivers that never reached the sea?
What diabolic plans justified your madness
So that you might create the dams of silence and death?
What evil order sustains your black architecture?
And now you are old.
Death lines up its guard, waiting for you.
You will be stretched out the complete millionaire.
Your fortune stolen between concubines and guns
Will remain here.
When you are rotting in your coffin
Your hens will go on pecking in the same hen house.
Perhaps a few will remember your cackling.
But the words of Roa Bastos
And many of your country
Will transcend the dams to become water
For the ocean and for the sky.

→←

Machismo

Boy of flesh and blood,
Now, a man of war
Forced to prove his manhood.

To us, yours
Is a brutal world,
Hard metals—
Machine guns,
Barbed wires,
Tanks,
Grenades,
Bullets,
Knives,
Mortar shells,
Shrapnel,
All designed
To rip to shreds and tear apart
The gentle fabric of human lives.

In all this hardness
No life, in a life
Lived on the line.

Heavy flak jackets,
Layers of body armor
Cover this soldier boy's
Thin skin,
His precious vulnerability,
His soft body
Covers his warm heart,
The tender cradle of his humanity.

Now all is covered
In steely, cold, hard armor
And the blood of mankind.

➤➤

مُفتــــاح الحَجَّـــة *The Key* מפתח ביתך

Dedicated with love to my mother, Rasmiya Hamed, may Allah,
God bless her soul, February 10, 1950–November 26, 2002

It's the story of a people
Looking for hope
It started on a day of war
Forced to leave their homes

The mother had to run
When the army used the gun
So she forgot to take her son
She was not the only one

The year was 1948
They established their state.
Now we have to fight and wait
Till we free our land

Now she's an old woman
Staying on her own
In a refugee camp
An old house made of stone

Where people carry hurtful stories
And happiness is gone
Where are your children?
I dared to ask.

She came back from the kitchen
The first is in the States
The second is in jail
The last one—hard to tell—

I lost him with Palestine
He doesn't know he's a son of mine.
Their father, where is he?
He was shot dead—

What do you have left?
Relax my son and listen to me
Taste some sweets
And drink your tea

Piece of steel
Made of hope
Hanging on the wall
Waiting to be dropped

It's my old key
To my orphan house
If my hope sleeps
My dream arouses

The hope, my son
Can see beyond time
Drink of the soul
Is in your blood like a wine

Tell me — who are you?
I'm an old guy — a young man
Looking for meaning among my people
In the search to find myself

Who is the child in the picture?
He used to gather friends
To tell them his plans
To fight against the army
Defending our land

Behind the olive tree he would hide
Throwing stones in his freedom fight
One stone hit a soldier
The soldier aimed his gun at our hero

The bullet hit him between the eyes
He fell beside the olive tree and died
His soul rose to heaven
All the village screamed and cried.

How can you forgive?
God forgives.
I try to forgive.
You must learn to forgive.

How can I forgive
When they took my land
I can't forgive
Can't you understand?

The stones of Mahmud
Made the army retreat
Now it's time to talk—
Peace will send them away

The stones of peace
Will return the holy Dome of the Rock
Free the melody of the bells
In the churches of the old city

Jerusalem will shine over Palestine
The time will come to work
To teach for freedom
To build our future

Love will call our sons home
You'll live, you'll give
Only then will you learn
To stop hating, start to forgive

I turned my face to the wall
And stared at the key
She cleaned the dust from her dream
And hung it over the photo of Mahmud.

I tasted some sweets
But they were so bitter
I tried to speak
But it was too hard . . .

→-

JAMES F. HARRINGTON

The Last Defender

For over three hundred years, the Russian Bear
wandered down from the cold north
to the warmer climate that beholds
the Northern Caucasus.

He ravaged anything that got in his path
in order to make the land safe for his kind.

To the Muslims of Chechnya
and other Caucasian nations
migration was the order of the day.

Many died because of this forced exile
Others survived hoping to drive the Russian Bear
out of their homeland.

Muslim Freedom Fighters kept the bear at bay,
prohibiting it from entering the capital of Grozny.

They fought against a most powerful enemy
inflicting much damage.

Until the last defender, atop a minaret,
died for his homeland and Islam.

⤚⤙

WALTER RENTSCHLER

From Fallen Heroes Will Arise

From Newark and Boston to New York, Washington,
and Pennsylvania. Cameras captured the epic flights,
the impact with sisters raped some years before
and the suddenness of it all aired on television over and over.
The silent sun saw it all.

It was a lovely day for flying, visiting grandchildren,
or just another business trip. Collapse!
Nothing is forever. All twins of the world must have shuddered.
The friendly skies of United were blue before they turned black.
What lay beneath? Heroes and what else? Staircase to safety,
a long way down. Dark. Some took the faster way.
Stairway to heaven.
The silent sun saw it all.

A new fear was born. We live with them all.
Our fears batten down the hatches.
We call out the National Guard, secure the airports,
guard power plants, patrol borders.
Homeland Defense. Yellow, orange, red, BANG!
Terror in, terror out. High alert, stand guard. Wave the flag.
Be brave. Big brother watches over us.
We watch each other. Check her ID. Search him. Report him!
We open our trunks before parking, we remove our shoes.
The silent sun sees it all.

Our leader says, "You're either with us or with the terrorists."
Afghanistan, Pakistan, Iraq, Iran, Armageddon.
God bless America. As easy as that.
Destroy and rebuild in our image.
And the silent sun will see it all.

➤➤

SAMUEL HAZO

Parting Shot

Nothing symphonic will come of this,
        nothing of consequence, and nothing
        to silence those whose business
        is creating funerals where widows
        in their twenties carry folded flags
        to empty bedrooms.
                      Pronouncers
        and announcers govern from their desks
        while corporals and captains pay
        the price in loss.
                I cite
        the history of Danielle Green.
She basketballed her way from poverty
to Notre Dame, played guard
with champions and honed a shot
she took lefthanded just beyond
the paint and rarely missed.

Later in Iraq a bomb
        exploded near enough to claim
        her shooting hand.
                   Others
        lost more, and many lost
        everything that anyone can lose.
Some say that poetry has other
        themes to sing about than that.
If that's the case, what good
        is poetry that shies away from pain
        and amputation?
                   What else can make us
        feel, not merely know, that severed
        limbs and lives can never
        be replaced?
                  And all for what?

➻

SIDNEY HALL, JR.

Imagine

A word from a song,
Printed brightly on a blue banner
Hung on the highest balcony.

Impossible to imagine
A war that has not begun,
A black-headed boy buried
Along with his soccer ball,
A young mother's broken breast
On a red sidewalk.

A word from a song.

Impossible to imagine
One quarter of a million people
In the streets trying to end
A war that has not begun.
Impossible to imagine the echo
Of incensed humanity
Twisting up the avenue
Between the white buildings,
Or the face of a man next to me in the march,
Under a thick blue hood,
Behind a grey beard,
Crying as secretly as he can.

--->--

BARBARA BALD

Walls

Resting on sage-green aquarium grasses,
the feathery red betta peers out
from his hexagonal glass tank.
Laying aside his Siamese reputation for fighting,
he stares at me from a watery world.

Questioning this fish's loneliness,
I recognize it as my own. I want to reach in,
invite him out for tea and cookies,
tear down walls built for protection,
walls that make it impossible for us to touch.

Lennon's words break my reverie, *Imagine*
there's no heaven, imagine there's no hell,
nothing to kill or die for and no religion too.

I recall times I've slammed doors in anger,
pouted off to some corner, turned my face
to mask my tears, avoided others'.
I think of arguments that curtail summit talks,
imprisonments that end dialogues,
bombs that silence.

Imagine all the people living life in peace.
Watching the betta hang at the top,
I sob into my teacup.

→→

CANDICE STOVER

Mantra for a New Year

"Choose a simple word," he said, "such as *God*.
Make sure you can say it in one breath.
Or chant it. Or hold onto it, for life.
Your tone of voice is everything: listen
to it turning God to grief, jokes, a curse.
Of course we all know men will kill for it.
(Which means, of course, not only men will die.)"

God. Rhymes with *clod*. Two *odds*. (*That awed clod, God.*)
Backwards, just a dog. Choose a simple word.
Then say it. *God*. We have to start somewhere.

→→

CANDICE STOVER

On the Burning and Looting of Iraq's National Library

Read now these ruins—
scorched translations of the word
made rubble. Sift ash
and sand for these voices torn
from history   a charred page   wind

➤➤

Desecrations in Fallujah

Many in the crowd were excited young boys
bent   on dragging bodies through the streets
to hang them, burnt, from the bridge like ruined toys.
Many in the crowd were excited. Young boys
rushed the cameras, chanting hate. Behind them, noise
of someone with a metal pipe on human flesh, beating
many. In the crowd were excited young boys
bent on dragging bodies. Through. The streets . . .

➤➤

Al-Fajr: A Military Offensive Named "Dawn"

Always after dark—
a warren of alleyways—
orange explosions
lighting the minarets—dust—
one man preparing the graves

➤➤

CANDICE STOVER

Page Four, August

Hot dark streets—checkpoint
where a boy shot dead still holds
his sister's body—
a mother wants to drink blood—
even the Alps are melting—

➻

Lungs

All day they're at it—
inspiring, filling us up—
baby's first breath, last
gasp of the tyrant, little
pink balloons taking on air.

➻

Who the Bomber Was

> The attacker, identified as Hiba Daraghmeh, 19 . . . was an English
> literature student, described as very devout by her father
> — AP news report

No telling what poems
she loved or carried   measured
words beneath her veil
the hour she strapped explosives
to her skin, then counted, *"One —"*

➻

Letter to the Generals Outside the City

I cannot feel rancor in the face of this great suffering.
— Thich Nhat Hanh

You cannot kill killing, through you find
the ones who do or will, the ones who dare
to bomb or hang torn bodies from a bridge. This mind
you cannot kill—*killing*—though you find
it (because we find it) everywhere. *What kind
of mind is it?* we ask. Statistics answer.

⇥

Meanwhile, on the Domestic Front

Sabrina humming
dices broccoli; red-haired Sal
slices onions thin.
Caps and stems of mushrooms part—
women peaceful between knives.

⇥

During the Invasion: Molly Joins the Spelling Bee

She draws "gazpacho"
first, then spells "belligerent."
Meanwhile, her sister
tries to sleep in a room sealed
against bombs, sounding out sky.

⇥

RICHARD CAMBRIDGE

Bad Weather

Our language comes from Arabic

There's a bin-Laden
For every letter of the alphabet

The forecast today
Is Bad Weather

A cluster bomb
In Copley Square

A suicide bomber
At Downtown Crossing

What doesn't rain from above
Can't be protected from with an umbrella

It's going to be a Nuclear Day
Mushrooms exploding in the corners of Everywhere

Lunch appointments completely ruined
A whole life's work blown to bits

My parents no longer exist
In Rochester

There's a fingernail left
Of a friend from Montana

What we need is
HOMELAND SECURITY

A T-Shirt says
Fighting Terrorism since 1492

Depicting four Native American warriors
Rifles cocked

What goes around
Becomes a tornado

Two-fifty for a coffee and donut
Two-fifty for a gallon of gas

The president grins
With a moustache of oil

Got Democracy
Wasn't it Sadaam who took down the towers

The forecast today is Bad Weather
It's always easier to believe a lie

➜➤

PAUL NICHOLS

Changed Perceptions

In my childhood
they were whirlybirds —
just silly whirlybirds
thumping through blue sky
with no serious connections.

I can't think of them like that anymore.

Now they're choppers.
I've seen them as precious
life saving medevacs one minute . . .
horrific attacking death dealers
the next.
Even their sound
faintly approaching from nowhere,
thundering overhead,
then disappearing on the horizon
has been forever transformed
from novelty to dread.

➜➤

SALLY SULLIVAN

Words Set Free

Why are words
so hard to find
today? Why don't they
just slip out
between the cracks?

Why not string
words on tinsel
or barbed wire?
Or shake them
up with vodka
and vermouth, then
pour them out for
people to enjoy?

Why not hurl words
like snowballs at the moon?
Or toss them gently
to a child who's learning
to play catch?

Why not let words
roll down like ticker tape
to festoon cars below?
Or let them sift
like pollen from white pine
on asphalt everywhere?

Why not plant words like grains
of corn to feed
a hungry world?
Why not make carillons of words
ring out a call
for peace?

→►

SALLY SULLIVAN

In the Bush Years

As I listen to reports
of atrocities by guards
against prisoners, I take
another bite of scrambled eggs
with parsley on whole-wheat toast.

I've forgotten how to feel.
In such dreams as I remember
I'm rearranging objects
or cookie cutter men.

At dawn my eyes devour
treetops filling out
with soft green leaves.

→-

BEVERLY ALMGREN

Pain

Yesterday at the dentist
I stared at the ceiling lights,
Memorized the pattern
As his fingers probed and pushed.

But there was no pain
Only the prick of the needle
And then, the blessed numbness.

When I was young,
Dentists hurt.

For some reason now I remember
The story of a scientist
Whose hundredth birthday was just celebrated

By a select few, remembering how his work was key
To the invention of computers and nuclear bombs.

He died a half century ago
Screaming in terror, it was reported
Not from the pain of the cancer that killed him,
But because his mind could no longer
Think its powerful thoughts.

In the dentist's waiting room
I read of a reporter's training
For going out with troops
To a war our country is about to start.

They learn, these reporters in the field,
About gas masks,
And how to deal with wounded combatants
They may encounter.

If the guts are spilling out, they learn,
Don't try to put them back.
Just pile them on top.

Have we now found numbness enough
To deal with this also?

→-

ELIZABETH TIBBETTS

Small Soup-Poem on a Day of Bombing

For Elise

Coconut milk
curry
cardamon, salt.
Chopped pumpkin
garlic, onion
kale. Exalt

the pot, spoon
blue flame
appetite.
Fill your bowl
with hot yellow
soup. Now eat.

➻

ELIZABETH TIBBETTS

Winter of 2003

Winter reared up from the past like a story
wanting to be told. Snow freshened nightly
until it reached mid-thigh. Thermometers
stuck at five below, while the last of the old
old recollected driving teams and sleighs

across lakes, the babies wrapped in robes,
and 1918, when they walked the frozen bay
eight miles out to the islands. We filled
the porch feeders, and mornings, watched finches
and chickadees blow in from the spruce

like good news to scrabble for seed. Sundays
we waxed our skis and followed the woods trail

that curved and dipped, then crossed a muffled stream
still running beneath snow, though the air was
so cold it seemed to crack. Everything white

and blue-shadowed, dreamlike. Flakes the size
of nickels drifted from lavender skies.
It was the hard winter we had longed for—
all ambition buried beneath the tasks
of shovel, firewood, and staying alive,

our worries tempered by muscle and sweat
into a sweet, heavy fatigue. We slept
so deeply, burrowed down below the days'
grim news, that when we woke
it seemed another way of being might still be.

➤➤

PRISCILLA F. SEARS

Rising

The sky is falling
In New York
And Washington
And Kabul
And Kirkuk.
Nothing rises
Except smoke
And ghosts.

But here in my kitchen
A fly struggles
In the leftover coffee
In the red cup
In the sink.
I lift her on the blade of a knife,

And hoping she won't fall,
I take her to the open window.
Still alive, she shortly revives
And flies away
Into that self-same sky.

→►

ANDREW PERIALE

Morning, April 2, 2003

5:45 A.M., and the rat-a-tat
of the old dog's toenails
on the hardwood floor above me
is all the alarm clock I need

to know that it is afternoon
on the desert and another marine
has been taken out by a patriot's suicide,
another mother caught in crossfire.

I pull on yesterday's underwear and look out at my van,
dusted with new snow like a patina of fine sand
on someone's Armored Fighting Vehicle,
or someone's eyes turned heavenward.

I'll eat scrambled eggs, drive down from the mountain,
work with seventh graders to make theater out of local history
while other children cannot sleep for
all the history being writ, and loudly, too.

The stiff-legged rat-a-tat upstairs
says, "Hey, get dressed! Come up for breakfast!"
while in Nasiriyah rat-a-tat yells: "Hey, get down!"
and tracer bullets are the child's night light.

→►

DEBORAH BROWN

For the Cousins

Forgive me for wearing a wool jacket this morning,
for eating eggs, and toast with plenty of jam,
for putting my feet up,
for reading this book of poems
in a house where no one will knock
with a warrant or a black boot.
And forgive me the luck of a grandfather,
a second son, who left Vilna, circa 1910,
his name garbled by an immigration officer
into the nicely English Towshire.
Forgive me, I say, for his luck, and mine.
He claimed his faith saved him. I replied:
"False Gods — and what about those cousins?"

Forgive me, cousins, the words on NPR
of a 15-year-old Albanian girl began this poem.
She will kill herself soon—her rape shamed her family.
On a street in Kabul, a doctor forbidden to practice
turns tricks. But what difference how long
I make this list? Cousins, I had forgotten you
until your eyes ignited in the faces of these others
and your voices sorrowed in their throats.

—✈—

DAVID BUDBILL

April 3, 2003

The end of winter: evening falling:
outside: the world is mud and rotten snow.
Inside: a little fire in the woodstove takes the chill away.
The kitchen: warm and comfortable.
Pasta, red sauce, wine and salad.
Some tinkling sounds in the evening glow.

After supper we lie together wrapped around each other
in the quiet evening, in the peaceful dark, this sweet silent.

What else is there to want except supper together,
a place to lie down and hold each other?

Half a world away, Dr. Saad al-Fallouji, the hospitals' chief surgeon, said
that just today the hospital received 33 victims dead on arrival
and 180 others who were wounded by American fire.

All of them were civilians, he said. *All of them were from Nadir village,*
women and children and men of all ages, mostly they had very serious
injuries to their abdomens, to their intestines, to their chests and their
heads. Many of the bodies were completely torn apart, he said.

→►

MEG BARDEN

Wishful Winter

Pines and spruce are frosted,
Fields filled with snow.
I want to cut that blanket
Into thousands of white strips.
Then send as flags of truce
To Fallujah, Mosul, Baghdad.

I want to gather baskets
Of sparkling stars from the night sky
And fly them to Iraq.
A glistening star will be awarded
To every soldier who will
Throw away his gun or defuse a bomb,
A golden star for peace.

→►

ANNIE FARNSWORTH

Lending My Breath

For the survivors

Tufts of grass blanch in the dust
while we've waited for rain that won't fall.
Then Tuesday, I felt it, like you did, something
else in the air. Not the promise of rain
nor proverbial nip of fall. Am I just now
noticing how wonderful it is to breathe?
how like nectar the air?
I drink it in, this sweet stir, knowing
what I have always known – that we
are with each breath taking in
atoms of the dead. Haven't we always
known this – haven't we been told
no matter is lost, but transformed?
And yet since Tuesday, the currents
have brought us two hundred and eighteen
floors of husbands wives children
all at once, and now I see
what an important job this is – how we must
breathe them in, let their molecules move
through our veins, through our bones,
since theirs have been spilled, crushed.
How we must cradle them within us,
so they are never really lost.

➤➤

PRISCILLA BURLINGHAM

What Happened to Childhood

Within the crumble
of World Affairs opinions
now are broken zippers
off the track
beyond repair

Kept from the knowledge of war
the child is allowed
to know the World is beautiful
there are no children
any more

My table's covered
with unread books
lovely barricades
some piled like stuffed animals
waiting to love

In the bunker
on the bed
I find my cats
one black one grey
sleeping yin and yang
pairing breath
and I remember
the World is beautiful

➤➤

EDITH N. CHASE

Peacemaking

Each person I meet
On the road of my life
Possesses potential
For peace or for strife.

How I treat such a person
Is likely to be
What makes him a friend
Or opponent to me.

Who, then, is responsible
Only God knows
When we see men or nations
Behaving as foes?

→⇥

CONNIE ROBILLARD

Voices of Peace

"A War to End All Wars," he said.
I snuggled softly in my bed.
My child voice whispered
Prayers of trust.
I believed in truth.

With flowers in my hair
I danced in the town square.
Holding a sign, "War is not
Healthy for children
And other living things."

My voice yelled, "Never again!"
I was young, my voice strong,
I believed I was heard.

I have lived
Through many wars—
Gathering wisdom
As I grow.
This is what I've come to know:

War is another name for shameful acts of violence
War whispers lies into the ears of youth
The people of conscience are on the street
Chanting, "Never Again!"

→⇥

JANICE SMITH SEUFERT

Memorial Day, 1865

The general's order was given.
This day will be designated
as a special time—
a remembrance, observance,
kept from year to year.

He could not have seen
the calumny, agony
of the century ahead.
The stilled roar of cannon's mouth
and end of that "late rebellion"
brought hope for peace.

On family farms, stones
of many sons were dressed.
No one dreamed of places
like Argonne, Aisne-Marne,
Guadalcanal, Heartbreak Ridge,
Tet or Normandy.

Now, in a New Hampshire cemetery,
we bring lilacs and bleeding hearts.
In Hawaii, the frangipani
and sweet pikake leis
rest on graves within the Punch Bowl.

We ask ourselves, our God,
where we could have found
a different road to take.
We wonder what another century
will bring—what brotherhood
or horror.

JANICE SMITH SEUFERT

Child of Sudan

Because I didn't want to see his eyes,
I turned my head—a simple move for me.
A picture given doesn't give the cries
or foul stench of disease. I wouldn't see
the hope gone out; yet something asking, still,
why hurt begins and never seems to end.
When did the loving stop? Just who will fill
the cups and mothers' breasts, or who will send
the rain and salve the wounds? Big people know
important things, big people have the might.
Where are their talents now? Where is the flow
of oil for human lamps that fail to light?
I couldn't let that look come close to touch,
so tried escape. Dear God, I care too much!

➤➤

MAREN TIRABASSI

Metanoia

I am not surprised—
by reckless kindness in victims
of tornado, wild fire, accident,
by the courage of cancer,
by the smile of a sleeping child,
any child,
by electric minds, passionate poems,
and long basketball muscles
of teenagers raised
in the harshest and poorest
circumstances.

I am not surprised—
by integrity in a politician,

forgiveness in an incest survivor,
excitement, unalloyed by cynicism,
in a forty-year teacher,
looking out at September faces,
by unnecessary compassion
in a parole officer,
bone-tired emergency room nurse,
taxi driver giving a free ride
in the snow.

Therefore, I cannot be surprised
by the graphic brutalities
of Abu Ghraib prison,
for I already believe
the truth of turning around —
the tide rushes to the empty shoreline,
tyranny
to the emptiness of America.

➤➤

NEIL ENGLISH

Distant Whir

A November dawn on Knubble Bay
and all the world is rising . . .
Flood tide rising,
red orb of sun rising
over the spine of Westport Island.

Then,
a distant whir
as crows also rise,

but whirring escalates,
from barely audible triple caw
through raspy insults hurled
to avian fiendish frenzy —

Crows convened in military tribunal.

Spiraling upwards now,
above the shore
and that still shadowed line of pine

then,
descending,
to mete out quick justice . . .

Death by pecking
for that one accused
of sleeping on watch
and missed alarm.

Oh dear God,
Master of this universe,

I pray that you have imbued these birds
with far greater intellect than man—

That every sentence handed down
be nothing short

of infallible.

→—

TESS BAUMBERGER

How dare the sky be blue today
instead of weeping red blood tears,
filling itself with purple clouds,
and thundering its grief
against keening heart of earth?

How dare the sun shine bright today
instead of hiding its yellow face,
vowing not to reveal rampant horror,
not to shine where it can no longer
warm the innocent dead?

How dare the mirror sea reflect traitor sun
instead of shrouding itself with black,
declaring a watery day of mourning?
How dare birds continue to sing?
How dare the spinning universe not pause?

How dare the world have beauty
instead of consonanting itself
with the ugliness of now?
At least Manhattan had
the grace to anoint itself with ash.

➤➤

JEFF FRIEDMAN

Memorial

For Gerald Stern

It's nice to remember the houses
floating on water. It's nice
to stand on shore and sing
a hymn of praise
while candles burn
in the windows.
It's nice to dream the loaves
rising in ovens
and the floors dusted with flour,
the women with beautiful
hair falling like cities
into darkness, the long
nights of love. It's nice to pretend
we could have saved them.
It's nice to say a few
words as spring turns to fall,
as fall turns to winter, and winter to spring.
It's nice to return again
and stare at the stars

so bright and forgettable.
It's nice to remember laughter
spilling into the wind,
roses sprouting from fleshy mouths
as children fall down
and down into the dirt.
It's nice to remember the voices
calling for you, calling
back the curtains, calling
through the long sleeves, the hollow places.
It's nice to remember the feast
of speckled blackbirds
huddled on the rims
of roofs, the stars
drawn in ash on the doorways,
the lament of uncles—
the long dance that kicked
up the dust and crinkled leaves,
the bodies waiting to burn,
the ash drifting on water.

→→

LIZ AHL

Walter Cronkite Takes Off His Glasses

Lunch at the sports bar, a dozen televisions
peer down at us: Abtronic® on one screen,
trivia on another; on a third,
another memorial service, dangerous mix
of grief and righteous self-congratulation—

Just give me Walter Cronkite
behind a desk
no made-for-TV-movie theme music
no made-for-TV-movie title graphic:
>   *Attack on America*
>   *America United*
>   *America Strikes Back: This Time, It's Depersonalized*

no Mondrian split screen,
no hired-gun expert analyst in one corner,
no bonus talking head in the other corner,
no ticker tape dragging along beneath,
no harried speculation to fill dead air,
no race for ratings—
just the story, and silence
when there's no more story—

Just Walter Cronkite,
one man, one head, no ticker tape—
all info, no 'tainment—

Just Walter Cronkite,
whose biggest dramatic flourish
was the occasional removal
of his spectacles
in grief or grinning disbelief:
  Kennedy shot
  Moon landing

Just Walter Cronkite
taking off his glasses,
maybe touching his forehead,
maybe shaking his head a little
before he pulls it together
and turns over the next page.

➤

CHARLES P. RIES

A Perfect Order

The elevator rises as another
   one descends.
Bill's son is ten and learning
   basketball.
The air smells of Fall days, cool
   nights and Harvest moons.
Mary's daughter is thirteen and
   pregnant.

I have fallen back in love with French
                bread and tomatoes.
My friend Steve just had his
                leg blown off in Iraq.
My life at middle age is finding its
                balance.

In an endless galaxy
                Amidst a vast sea
                                I sit in a small boat
                                                And try to figure out
Which way the wind is blowing.

→>—

Burton Hersh

Why the Eagle Screams

It pumps me up that ours is a nation with a glint in its eye,
Infused with a vision, the way our pastor puts it.
Or is that desperation? Sparks off our mission in the world?
Emanations from our irritable bowel?

I have to ask, who queered our compass this time around?
How could a culture this shallow get in so deep so fast?
Our dim future mortgaged to one more generation of Hottentots
Who hate us worse this time than last time we saved their souls.

Not that Old Europe is surprised, particularly.
Our sputtering dog-faced Commander, compassionate beneath his laurels,
Arfing through his phrase book, Anubis, triumphant in war.
Was this the citizen-ruler Jefferson had in mind?

Meanwhile, halfway around the planet, urchins languishing in the dooryard
Of the mosque are enveloped by our incendiary accomplishments,
Our attention from seventy-five-thousand feet, which leaves them . . .
Transfigured. With their skins unfurled.

All this for reasons it has become confusing
To pretend to remember.

→>—

GEORGE V. VAN DEVENTER

A Soldier's Birth

I' crime and enmity they lie
Who sin and tell us love can die
        — From "Born upon an Angel's Breast," John Clare (1793–1864)

To love is to give your self away
        like a mother
                when her child is called to arms.

Every soldier has a mother defended by a child.

You'll find no argument from me that love is strange.

Desperate to please love gives up its body,
        the inner me that orders up a cup of coffee
                and dreams that women are like trees—comforting.

Trees have deep roots and a thirst quenching shade.

I'll cut a tree as quick as kill another man
        for love of home, god and country.
                There's no doubt love can drive a person mad.

It seems as though love's a painted image over glass—
        an icon, if you like, staring in on me
                as silent as the wind outside from where I stand.

You'd think I'd take a rag and wipe my window clean,
        see behind and beyond the face of love
                in those that waved me off to war.

When the tree fell I took it as mine
        and turned to see
                mother waving merrily at me.

→→

JOY STARR

Skimming the Cream

In two zero two four
Where will we be
If every twenty years
We breathe war?

We recruit our noblest and best
To survive an ultimate test
And dare Darwin as never before.

Our youth in their prime
Get sent to the line
To settle a political score.

We lose the best in their prime
With offspring in time
To fight in twenty forty-four.

A warring nation breeds
A lost population
Of soldiers who will never be born
Or know the wounds of war.

➤➤

STEPHEN WING

The Money Missing from Our Paychecks

We who eat
lest we grow hungry, we who
lie down to sleep
because we know to the minute
what time we rise,

              a bomber is blinking
across our bathroom mirrors that does not sleep,
a sentry walks the perimeter of our dim bedrooms

till the alarm rings
and we reach out to stop it

A truckload of soldiers comes leaping out
into smoke and noise when we
tear open our paychecks every Friday in the bar,
a bomb drops away from the black wing
even while we curse
with ritual laughter the government
which has siphoned our blood in the night again
to fuel helicopters and tanks

A distant flame is casting those faint shadows
on the TV screen, a burning
that does not stop for Happy Hour,
while the bodies untangle from the pileup
and the referee bends to retrieve a fumble,
the family scattered
by an American bomb does not get up

The bodies are brown
as the football
waiting at the scrimmage line again, but broken
like the field they farmed

They are too busy giving their
blood back to the soil
to blame us, but it is our slow suffocation they fight
for every breath, the money missing
from our paychecks every Friday has bought us
the pumping of their hearts
to dip our chips in and wash down
with our beer
                It is our war
and only our waking hands can reach out
to stop it

➤➤

MAXINE KUMIN

Purgatory

And suppose the darlings get to Mantua,
suppose they cheat the crypt, what next? Begin
with him, unshaven. Though not, I grant you, a
displeasing cockerel, there's egg yolk on his chin.
His seedy robe's aflap, he's got the rheum.
Poor dear, the cooking lard has smoked her eye.
Another Montague is in the womb
although the first babe's bottom's not yet dry.
She scrolls a weekly letter to her Nurse
who dares to send a smock through Balthasar,
and once a month, his father posts a purse.
News from Verona? Always news of war.
          Such sour years it takes to right this wrong!
          The fifth act runs unconscionably long.

➤➤

J. KATES

Shakespeare in the Bush Administration

Francisco in the pay of Fortinbras,
destabilizing Denmark, brings the prince
by means of well disseminated hints
into an open conflict with his class,
into disillusionment, despair
and dialectical loquacity
matched only by the incapacity
of king and court to deal with this affair.
No wonder we go mad, and more than mad,
some of us going underground, some reaching
too far after one more silly flower
or unripe fruit just hanging to be had,
some of us spouting all the stoic teaching
we soaked up in Philosophy 104.

➤➤

WILLIAM HEYEN

Horns

When their army unpacked to remain here,
their goods were stacked halfway up our mountain.
Our sure-footed sheep peered at crates and artillery with interest,

but kept their distance, making new paths to avoid the soldiers.
The sheep nor we knew how long these occupiers would be here
with their atrocities and chocolate bars,

but the rams' horns did not curl into this question,
the ewes' rhythms did not falter, and lambs were born,
though there were losses to drunks at target practice.

During the day, we farmed, at night we sharpened our knives
and welcomed smugglers with news from other villages.
They told us the foreigners, though well supplied for now,

were stretched thin, and the wolves were at their heels.
They told us to wait another winter. They asked, with a wink,
if any sheep had consorted with the enemy.

--->--

DAMON GRIFFIN

New, New Apocalypse

Subtle as a bomb, I am tapped
in to the truth about these
dark goings-on.

We are friends, I guess.
I think you were drenched
by a wave of cheap charm.
You could fool a whole nation.

And when the fright strikes
and the cash is right,
I am supportive.
I help you chase that unholy tail.

When the beams begin to dim,
people stand still, pay attention.
What am I to do
but stand with them?

You say: this is the situation:
help in the struggle for annihilation
of the dust bitten, the hell-children.

If I fall, your hands will catch my back.
You will stop my death in its stride.
You see a menace
coming around the block.

"It wants to abuse us," you cry,
"and weld scars in our skin
and it won't stop coming. Attack!"
The lies you spit out are soft as razors.

It's a clever way to end the world;
a brand new apocalypse we share.
But while it erupts, I can rest at home.

You're no friend of mine.
You want to chew power
to crack my spine.

You just want more
Hands to build your temples.
The menace is you,
cutting my skin.

You spark a thousand
torches from the flames in hell,
you laugh at train wrecks,
you ring false bells.

As light as a brick, you
smile at a holocaust.

ASKIA M. TOURÉ

American Nightmare 1: Vampires

To Colin and Condi

Black people gone "Corporate," allowed back seats
in the butcher-shop of the Vampire's cannibal
Lair. The Liar, the Monster, no longer called Count
Dracula (that's too foreign, too medieval, too bizarre);
no, call him Vic or Ric, and her Bunny or Buffy, both
blond, Germanic and beautiful: model Aryans, lawyers,
like Allie McBeal, producers, super-models, blond,
Germanic wunderkinds . . . though "troubled," being
Privileged among the Homeless, the castrated blacks
and Latinos, leaves one "troubled," though rich and
regal, with Ken and Barbie among the Vampires and
sycophants of the American Nightmare, known
as "Freedom," . . . where Texas Oil megabucks buy
the White House, jail welfare moms, while Lonely
Crowds wander aimlessly among spinning Game Show
wheels, composed of the bones and sinews of dead
"Redskins" . . . American Dreams for sale among the
Vampires and Sycophants; naked images of
J. Edgar Hoover, perfumed, in drag, masquerading as
Marilyn Monroe, with dress blown up, exposing
panties and bandy, hairy legs . . . Corporate suites
sleuth through the night, as "Men in Black" killing
"X-file" idealists, taking Fox Mulder as paradigm.
American Dreams for sale, haunted by slain prophets:
Martin's regal voice ringing in the future; Malcolm's
volcanic fury exposing Vampires, echoing in hurricanes
from Africa whirling through ravaged country-sides.
American Dreams slaughtered, like the Kennedys,
and "John-John," while Bush-whacking Vampires
create coups, "Shock and Awe" Apocalypse, goose-
stepping across borders of a Dark & frightened World!

➤➤

ETHAN GILSDORF

Breaking News

"We go now live to Barbieville, where Ken
is standing by. Ken?" "Here in Barbieland,
a brother has wantonly crossed the long-tolerated
'invisible line' demarcating his end of the den
from his sister's. Advancing his Hummer 248
(with Bushmaster) past the toy box to the edge
of the Afghan blanket, the brother dared to crush
the dinette set and plush snake protecting
the up-until-now untouchable
Barbie Grand Hotel and Talk-and-Shop
Supermarket complex. An elite guard
of Beanie Babies and a pile of preschool blocks
were also no match for his superior firepower,
assisted by a wooden mallet and Pokemon doll.
But, in a remarkable reversal of fortune,
when the invading forces reached the Barbie
stronghold, the brother and his Bushmaster
were beaten back by, what, I'm sorry? Yes,
panty hose, nail polish and lipstick.
The brother was quoted as saying, 'Ew! Gross!'
as he retreated from a cloud of hairspray
back across the imaginary line,
a little hint of rouge in his cheekbones.
Barbie was sighted earlier fleeing
the shopping center for Surf City in her
Jam 'n Glam Tour Bus, but reports now
confirm her glorious return to Barbieville,
accompanied by her multinational clones
who are reportedly fellow partygoers.
This is Ken, reporting live from
the Afghan blanket. Now back to you.
No, wait, we're going to commercial."

➤➤

Risk®

"The game of global domination™"

Born from manufactured casts, plastic foot soldiers fill the box.
Each is called an army: the thing they represent on the game board.
I ask if, by house rules, we can just call them men,
They're so tiny that two or three might fit inside a thimble.
My color for the game is black, Momma's is red (her favorite)
Pop's is blue and Christopher's is green.

The first round claims initial territories.
My tactics are random. Momma goes to places she'd like to visit.
Pop decides on North America, he grabs the U.S. first,
Declaring, they can't be defeated.
Christopher starting in South Africa moves north and east. Strategy.

A generational battle can be seen: the father against the lover.
For the elder it is patriotism and loyalty to win the wars,
But youth has tenacity and vigorous logic.

From the start Christopher knows when to roll and when to retreat.
He eats up the African continent, covering it with little green men.
Then he claims South America and seeps into Europe.
Momma cares only to defend Scandinavia, her motherland.

My men soon stand as the underdogs, thirty down to five,
In China the Pacific Islands and Ontario.
We alternate between laughter and grunts of frustration as we roll.
I begin to think, as I hold my borders through chance and luck,
That perhaps this game is a set of tarot cards in disguise.
The patterns of color are rearranged as Pop and I are pushed out.
Christopher conquers, knowingly and confident.

Pop and I are grumpy with defeat and each storms off to bed.
Momma's strongholds grow through blissful and ignorant luck.
A perpetual beginner, she is cheerful even when her borders fall.
A few green men are flicked back to the kitchen table, off the board.

From upstairs I can hear Momma's sharp, quick laugh
And Christopher's emphatic "HA!" I picture his finger pointing.

Over and over the dice clatter lightly on the game board.
I come back down after an hour, pajamaed and ready to flip the game over,
Scattering little plastic men all over the floor.

→→

KATHERINE SOLOMON

Pentagon Fantasy

*In 1993, in Indonesia, vibrations imperceptible to human ears were recorded
on the slopes of volcanic Mt. Semeru, seismic vibrations of "extraordinary
character, notable for their striking regularity."*
                                        — Geophysical Research Letters

Deep in Mt. Semeru, earth-heart beats
with a rhythmic pulse. Scientists say there must be
a logical cause, one that obeys all the currently-known
geophysical laws; but I say who knows
what laws might in the end connect
reason and phenomena? And who can say

our perfectly logical set of local laws
doesn't have a corollary that allows the earth
to have a heart? The eavesdropping scientists believe
it's magma interacting with an empty channel: something
roughly like the deep vibration made by blowing across
the top of a small-necked bottle. I'll never hear
the tune Mt. Semeru is playing. My ears
aren't fashioned to receive that sound. But listen:

Before a day last winter, I'd never seen a star-
shaped snowflake either, a pure pentangle like the gold ones
sister Mary Albertine used to stick on my forehead
when I recited the catechism lesson perfectly, each word
falling into its sing-song slot. It happened

in the car, as I blindly poked the key at the ignition,
and stared with unfocussed eyes through the windshield:
half a dozen perfect, five-point snowflake stars—five points,
I swear: not six the way they're supposed to be—like tissue-paper
cutouts, a slice of story book sky on a slide. But we all know
there's no such thing as a five-pointed snowflake. No such thing
as a star-shaped star in the sky.

Sometimes it seems only the very young
or those who've almost come full-circle, who've seen more
wonders than we dream of in our sober middle years, believe
in the possibility of anything. We live mostly on the level ground
of years when we are sure we've seen or heard of everything.

But once, in the time of extended belief I think of as my flower-
childhood, I fell asleep with a book about the pyramids
open like a roof above my heart, and dreamed about the shapes
of cities and buildings: imagined

how those constructions, like receptor cells
for hormones, viruses, and enzymes, lay open
to whatever galactic germ
would fit them. And I wondered
what cosmic energies our constructs might be calling
with their shapeliness and what they might repel.

War was raging then in Vietnam, and for a while
I felt certain we could stop it by changing the shape
of the Pentagon, that amputated star, that power
sink that seems to draw destruction down. It seemed we might
tack on five triangles and turn
that crooked circle into a star. Inside a delineated star,
who could think of anything but peaceful
and elegant solutions to aggression?

In just a weekend we could add on woven V-shaped walls
of willow wands and hazel, hang them with locks
of baby hair, bits of bread, baseball caps, and keys
to our apartments and our cars, wedding rings and strips
of our favorite old coats and dresses, our uniforms.

We'd make a new shape there
that would shine on the face of the planet to signal
some kind of transformation to whatever gods
might be looking, that would invite an infection
of affection. Regenerate
all our parts: body, soul, spirit, mind,
and heart. I thought we might
learn to listen to the earth
heart   beat.

EUGENE ELANDER

The Tape That Won the West

The prospects for terrorism,
Against the Land of the Free,
Used to really scare
The daylights out of me.
I feared those suicide bombers,
And planes hijacked in flight;
Thoughts of anthrax and smallpox
Haunted my sleep at night.

But now I have an answer,
Which surely works for me;
That answer came directly,
From Washington, D.C.
Our Security Officials
Say, "Forget all that black crepe:
Instead, protect your family,
With a roll of plain duct tape."

Now, duct tape's good for many things,
As any fool can see;
But duct tape defeating terrorism?
Well, that was news to me.

When I first heard this good news,
It seemed grasping at straws—
But now I know how duct tape works,
To serve our nation's cause.

Indeed, I really praise this tape,
Which won America's West,
When a Sheriff or U.S. Marshall
Pulled a roll from out of his vest.
Even good old Patrick Henry,
Stated, all in one breath:
"When it comes to Freedom,
Give me duct tape, or give me death."

But one need not review history,
To praise the Tape That Binds,
For now it's known that duct tape
Can change people's hearts and minds.
Even Osama Bin Laden
Who, just the other day,
Told his Al Qaeda network
Duct tape just won't go away.

And as for North Korea,
With its strong atomic threat,
Not to mention other nations –
Well, duct taped they will get.
Let's see them launch those missiles,
Let's see them even try –
With missiles taped to launching pads,
They'll never reach the sky.

The Age of Duct Tape's already here,
You'd best not make a fuss;
For there are but two choices:
You're with us, or against us –
The World must speak with one voice.
And that voice must be praising
America's Fearless Leaders,
No matter how much Hell they're raising.

So rest assured that duct tape's
The answer to every prayer;
Yes, we'll defeat our enemies,
No matter here, or there;
And so, though once I worried,
Now I know that foul is fair;
Indeed, I feel completely safe
Sitting duct taped to my chair!

-+-

BURKHARD HOENE

small talk

Journal entry, September 12, 2001

I'm thinking
the world is on fire
and I'm making small talk
in the middle of it all

We walked 60 blocks to get to a party
that I'm afraid to say was interesting
I thought it might be good
to get some exercise away from the TV

Life is grand, when you're depressed
the world has become the manic depressive
now we have to find a cure

There is something spiraling
dangerously out of control
as mankind busily
goes about work and play

I find myself becoming insensitive
just to protect myself
what am I afraid of?

What comes next
when the doors shut in front of me?
Where is the door
when the wall goes crack
and the building collapses in a cloud of dust?

ashes to ashes, dust to dust

→-

BURKHARD HOENE

what package is this?

Journal entry, September 23, 2001

What package is this
sent to us
from some far-away land?
sent by a messenger
yet without a message.

perhaps we sense uselessness,
cascading down the wire
from a local television channel

just who are we when we become
a media mind?

what is it
that builds the power
of such a country as ours?

similar resources, similar
television, similar people,
similar topography.

yet we have become the
cause and barometer of how
the world feels about itself.

is this the open society?

what is an open society
when it behaves as we do?
what values do we accept
and what values do we
impose on ourselves?
what values do we impose on others?

can we remain
indifferent?
can the blind remain
indifferent?

forgive them for
they know not what they do

➤

BURKHARD HOENE

a cold wind

Journal entry, October 7, 2001

a cold wind
has picked up across America.

we busy ourselves
with the mundane tasks of daily life
and begin to realize
that we have been missing something
along the way.

I wonder if I have prepared myself
sufficiently for this wind
descending upon us today.

is there a lesson
in these dark clouds in an unseen storm?

are we unlearning, in one month,
the lessons of human rights
and of equal opportunities for all
that we have worked, for decades,
to understand?

I pray that we may be open
to the changes
that this wind may demand of us,
that we will act honorably
and in accordance
with a love for our fellow man
and our fellow spirits

for the territory over which we fight
is now becoming increasingly the territory

of our good will
of our conscience

and of an understanding
of our neighbors
no matter where or how they may reside.

➤➤

BURKHARD HOENE

bangbang

Journal entry, April 5, 2003

the man
hears the news about his secretary of defense's warning
alluding to the invasion of two more countries

or the opening of a fourth world war
according to the way a former intelligence official put it

he smiles and continues about his papers

upon a second thought
he calls the bearer of news back into the room and says

Good.

not exactly the big bang
but it makes you wonder who's controlling the ship
wonder what the motivation is
behind this swelling tempest

they don't want to talk about it yet
the world might not take it so well
catch them while they are sleeping?

fake a pass and run?
deceive and pillage?
thing with thieves is
they never know when to stop

a rolling scenario of
wag the dog

we'll have to look further
than we have ever looked
to see the light at the end of this tunnel.

It's another Hail Mary
open up the pearly gates
and
while you are at it
Hail Caesar

➤➤

To Breathe the Least Bit of Fresh Air

On the fifth day of summer in the middle of the afternoon under a stone lion sweating the last of its magma steam the young woman from Martinique eased into shadows of buildings as if they were the shade of trees, then disappeared before northern eyes. The tailor of the men's clothing store, Ari, stepped out for a moment with a thread on his pants, a thread on his jacket, which he removed, both threads spinning him around until he must have stood there on the sidewalk, naked & cool. The woman reappeared out of the brick, out of the granite in her dress of blue water. In the parking lot of *Il Panino* a waiter left orange peels on the hood of his Volvo, while talking with two women, adding a sense of green absent from the pavement. Yet amid all this Peace, this collection of habits from home, the harsh reality of trouble underground, back on the subway where four Jewish kids with tennis rackets strewn all over the car floor talked in front of a man reading the Koran, the man reserving an extra seat for the Koran, glances of hate tossed at the boy in the yarmulke, which I witnessed when he tried to stare me down but my eyes wouldn't lower, & all three Gods, adamant in the corner of the car couldn't devise a way to breathe the least bit of fresh air into a sticky political situation.

-→-

Its Mission

Chaos plummeted, swirled through a funnel to the street I walked on: fire engine roared & sirened, two ambulances sped & sirened, damn, the look of panic in people's eyes! When all of a sudden the magnolia on St. Stephen Street in Boston quelled everything. Its just-awakened blossoms, without a tinge of bronze discoloring from the cold, rose, rose up ready to become the world's candelabra. In the middle of the night NATO should transplant it to the center of Pristina, Kosovo, watch the miracle of its mission. I should know. Last night two women called from each end of the corridor of the dream. One waved, "Shalom." The other, entering, thanked me for keeping everything picked up, saying, "Work is a form of worship."

-→-

When Time Is No Solution

That's exactly what I'm doing today, walking around in my head, not surprised to find that the letter "L" shaped like a leg rose up 3,000 years ago out of Palestine. Head. Dark corridors. Cul-de-sac. Myriad stones strewn over the open road. It's frightening when time is no solution. Last night she dreamt we bought a huge console clock at an estate sale. When carrying it out, jewels suddenly appeared on the wooden case. But today the quality of personal time is no consolation. There are men who love war. She told me last week she stumbled upon "labyrinth" in the dictionary, close to the word "labia." Absence of woman is a cause of war. The current political landscape of Palestine is a time without presence, covered with men without legs to stand on, a territory like the labyrinth, ancient enigma named after the double ax.

--->--

Can You Get the Sense of the Weight of a Gun from the Movies?

The day before we praise warriors in November, leaves from adolescent trees on the sidewalk on Mass. Ave. look as if stars fell overnight. In mourning. Kids in Kosovo, just north of the Cursed Mountains already curtained with snow, warm hands over steel boxes half-full of coals. It's reported the enemy took a motor from a sewing machine as an imbecilic act of sabotage, threw porcelain cups out of a school window with the genius velocity of light. I know of a young female runner made of bronze in 560 BC found in Albania. Why is she looking backward with such trepidation? Why lift her skirt to keep it from getting entangled at the knee? Why one breast out from tunic? How far are the Balkans from the strife of ancient times?

--->--

ROBERT GIBBONS

First Snow of Winter

No filming commercials or coining slogans at the abandoned Coke factory
on the outskirts of Sarajevo. The first snow of winter filtering through open
beams in the roof, witnessed by a thousand Albanian refugees attempting to
sleep during a crescendo of coughs. It's too crowded to add another stove
burning fragments of freight pallets. Cases of bronchitis, fever, diarrhea. In
bed, in winter boots & ski parkas, children whose mothers dare wash only
their faces. Western executives are keeping an eye on the situation, knowing
industry stockholders are a patient lot, & that these people can't hold out
forever. Someone ought to bottle tears of anguish. Target offspring of the
well-to-do. Then call it too priceless to sell.

--→--

LOIS FRANKENBERGER

The World According to The New York Times

Tiffany gold pendant hangs on silk cord
on the upper right
opposing ethnic Rwanda killings still unpunished
on the lower left;
Nigerian mother sentenced to death by stoning
on the upper left
shuns Chanel black & white high heel oxfords
on the lower right—

"Step into our new world" beckons the shoe

as Israel, on high alert,
hunkers down to celebrate the New Year;
while fire bombers paint
a German memorial museum's walls
with "the Holocaust is a lie"

and financial advisors say
"Bell South will rise again."

You may say "this is not my world"—

This absurd crossing into
some new Hell
where ordinary people are not yet
ready to dwell.

--->->

Samuel Hazo

Skunked

Alamo, Great Wall or Maginot—
    they all were breached, bypassed
    or broken.
                Generals like Foch
condemned such barriers as futile
and extolled attack.
                     But somehow
all attackers fail when conquests
burgeon into burdens, and the once
defeated waken and prevail.
Thucydides and Hemingway implied
    we're worse in war than beasts
    who only kill from need and never
    with malice.
               Are we that base?
Is strength the vice we copy
    from the lion?
               Guile from the fox?
Deception from the leopard?
               Stealth
    from the wolf?
            Or is this listing

too selective since it overlooks
    the sane and self-reliant skunk?
He keeps his enemies at bay
    and lives untouched in peace
    by smelling worse than awful.
In brief, he stinks.
                But still
    his odor scuttles the bother
    of battle and shows the perceptive
    how stench might serve as a perfect
    weapon of choice for the bullied—
    bloodless, inexpensive and effective.

➻

DIANA DURHAM

Colors of the Tiger

Black, gold
colors of the tiger

Black, gold
oil in the desert

Black, gold
hedgerows round the cornfields

Black, gold
dark space and solar flares

Black, gold
the power and the throne

Black, gold
the unknown and the known

Black, gold
The colors of the heart.

➻

J. KATES

How Can There Be a War Going On?

How can there be a war going on
when the window I look out is suffused
in morning sunlight, and one tall pine
after another marches into the drowsy
distance? Where is this so-called war?

Certainly not here. Certainly no one
I know squats under the scream and wheeze
of artillery, trembles with a premonition
of ambush just over the next sandy rise
or steers with skill the heavy machinery of war.

And no one I know cowers underground
and counts seconds between the whining throes
of falling bombs, holding close the children—
A word which by itself cries out pathos of peace
and the absolute calamity of war.

Oh, look! A funny squirrel has found the corn
we left for finches to eat. And overhead, crows
circle, take off and land freely all around.
Somewhere far away there is an indistinct noise—
traffic along a busy highway. Not war.

➤➤

J. Kates

REST 8.6.8.8.6

Some birds are preditors at day and pray at night.
— Shiran Goldner, 4th grade, Nashua, N.H.

O Lord of forest, lake and field,
        Of raptor and of rapt,
We are the killer and the killed,
By daylight hunters in the wild,
        Still learning to adapt.

O wind and wing of our belief,
        You know each sparrow's fall,
Great overshadow, tree of life,
Protective, stern, eternal cliff,
        And shelter for us all—

O Lord who, watching over us,
        Designed the falcon's flight,
Forgive the hunger of our days,
The tickle in our blood-stained claws,
        And keep us safe tonight.

→→

J. KATES

After One War

A grouse goes off
like a landmine.
I take the blow
full in my breast,
step backward
against rocks
laid down
millennia ago

by a smart glacier
precisely *here*,
and weep bitterly
for the quick deer,
the displaced fox,
the white birch
trembling overhead
in the gentlest
of breezes.

→→

DAVID ROMTVEDT

Gone

Boom, goddamn it, the bomb,
that invaded my sleep and waking,
the noise I can't describe,
my secret life, clicking and hissing,
the moments of deepest pleasure,
the sucking as air disappears from space.

I look down on my daughter's face as she sleeps.
She is more emissary than gift.
There is a union that each of us has with the other.
There is a real you reading this poem.

That was the bomb that rose
over the horizon line of my life—
the liver color, the mushroom cloud,
the river of fire, the invisible death to come,
the underworld bomb, the devil bomb,
the radioactive-cockroaches-take-over-the-kitchen bomb,
the planet-lifting-and-hung-upside-down bomb.

Now I live with the circus bomb, the carnival
sideshow bomb, the clown bomb, the cream pie
in his hand, he winds up and throws and when it hits

me in the face, or misses and hits my neighbor, the
ha-ha bomb, an explosion of laughter. By saying this,
I don't mean the bomb's less real.

It's just faith, or hope, an intuition
that things will be alright, that inside
the creamy filling there is a knife,
and though the blade is open and ready to cut,
it's not to kill us but to warn us, so we will wake.

→►

MARTIN STEINGESSER

The Disappeared

I heard about a woman of El Salvador
whose tongue was cut out
                              for asking after her daughter,
one of the disappeared in her village.
She asks us, "Where in the dust
have they flung my daughter
                              or my tongue?"
I am mindful how
                    my thoughts about her circle.
The summer night is loud with stars, and there is music
and clapping just down the road. Somewhere
the other side of night, my own daughter
is waking. I don't know on what her eyes light
when they open, only that the birds
                              surely sing in them.
Standing now under the astonishing stars, I think—
In what tongue does one summon daughters?
Sure as words spin out,
the birds this morning fly in my daughter's eyes.

→►

BAT-CHEN SHAHAK

A Summary of War and Peace

Dedicated to those whose light went out and are buried in the earth

There is not much left to say
We're in a sort of halfway spot.
Nor is there 'real war'
And we, we're marching forward towards peace:
Ready to understand the others,
Prepared to make changes,
With one clear goal:
To be rid of the hatred
Buried deep inside us for so long,
And with the understanding
That it's easy to make enemies,
But the wise thing is to find friends.

We are people who know a lot about war
But very little about peace.
From now on we'll begin to change that.
Behind the fine words are years and years
Of suffering, pain, anxiety and fear.
Now to all these words
A new word—*hope*—is added:
A little strange, a little different, perhaps.
In fact it was with us all along
(Even in war)
And because of it we never remained alone in the struggle.
If we talk about peace, we cannot conclude
Without the song that became the hymn of peace,
Together with the hope in our hearts
That remained with us all our lives.

➝➤

Bat-Chen Shahak

A Dream of Peace

Every person has a dream.
One wants to be a millionaire—
Another, a writer.
And I have a dream
About peace.
Sometimes we give up
On the special day
When everyone will be happy and united—
Right and Left,
Arabs and Jews—
And become partners and friends
And there will be no hatred and war anymore.
Maybe I'm a naïve girl
But is it too much
To ask for peace and security?
Is it too much to dream
Of waking securely
In the streets of the Old City?
Is it too much to ask
Not to see the mothers of
Young soldiers
Crying on their graves?

➤

poem to peace

Peace is a kind of dream
that holds only good things.
It's an easy life with no complications,
because peace means
there are no enemies,
and you're not appalled
all over again, each time
another awful attack happens.

➤

BAT-CHEN SHAHAK

Three Shots

In memory of Yitzhak Rabin

Three shots and it's all over—
Now we talk about him in the past tense.
Suddenly, the present becomes the past,
And the past is only a memory.
We are standing, crying,
We want to believe it never happened,
That it is all a nightmare,
And when we wake up the next morning—it will not be so.
Instead, we wake up to a warped reality,
Where pain is laced with hate.
We cannot digest the enormity of this loss,
And we cannot comprehend its severity.
How can we understand such a tragedy
In a civilization and not in the jungle?
Each one of us holds an opinion,
Yet, we do not have to agree.
We cannot turn back the clock,
But we can stop for today and remember.
For in a few days we will return to normality,
While the family is left to cope
With this abomination!
It is like that first fallen domino,
That provokes a chain reaction.
We were beheaded, in every sense,
And now it all crumbles.
As though he were the head, and we the body,
And when the head does not exist—the body dies!
It is impossible to build with parts that do not fit,
It is impossible to build with mismatched bricks.
It is an art to build a straight tower,
But a single kick can shatter it all.
And then,

One can destroy a State!
I do not understand the search for the guilty;
I think we are all guilty for not showing how much we loved him.
Like the children who grow up,
And only then understand their parents,
And sometimes it is too late . . .
They ask for forgiveness, they write and they cry.
Maybe I am too naïve
But I cannot understand
How so many people
Take the law into their own hands!
How can we take the best gift ever given—
Life.

We are all one.
We share the same fate,
Old and young.
We stand grasping each other
And we cry . . .
It seems even the essence of life
Is but little next to your greatness.

➤

MARYLIN LYTLE BARR

Challenge to a Warrior Nation

Inspired by W. H. Auden's "September 1, 1939"

Yes, we have survived
cataclysmic times
in our own history.
Now, let us gather
as "Ironic points of light"
sending sustenance
to survivors
of earthquake and flooded lands
food to the starving
healing medicine to the sick
ceasing the devastation we ignite.
Let us defy
our war machine shining
"an affirming flame"
fulfilling our human potential
become lights in darkness.

➤➤

JULIA OLDER

Soundings

In the shower I sand my heels
with volcanic pumice stone,
rubbing away the calluses
and spurs that slow progress
on this eruptive earth.

I close my eyes
and enter the molten stream.
There's nothing to it,
just a bright flow
of what matters:

The blue dragonfly
catching light on a stem.
The brave orange eft
on her maiden voyage
to Otter Brook.

The active baby
in its mother's arms
whose gaze is so
innocent of guile
it glows.

This epicenter
has at least
three full breaths
without a hint
of aftershock or fear.

→→

KATHERINE TOWLER

In Years to Come

In this time of days given too quickly
to the dark, snow hides what we believe
to be true. From the house to the car,
from the shed to the wood pile, we carve
a labyrinth where footsteps find prayer—
the frozen track we walk each morning in our refusal
to imagine the inevitable, in our numb hope
that one bomb might be stayed, one child
snatched from ruin. In years to come, will we say
this is where I stood when the war started—
at the end of the driveway, shovel in hand,
looking for another people,
looking to another land.

→→

PATRICIA RANZONI

Another War Spring

Deep woods meditation

(If we could only dam the lies
        we could hear the melt
        down the mountains.

If we could but still the guns
        we could hear the ferns
        begin their rise.

If we could confess harm
        we could hear the green
        greener than it's ever been.

If we could replace the greed
        we could hear the snow
        returning to our source.)

->-

PATRICIA RANZONI

Hearings

It's true, icicles formed through February could be the frozen paths
of bullets and bombs fired to kill any chance of what could be decided
about a stove with mutual regard and health. Without greed.
If enough will just keep willing! Is that it?

Through my bones tired concentrations resound.
Snows storm the whole way from before recorded time.
Whole peoples have vanished from distorted will
including faith we elder ones know the smell.

Silences becoming languages are the loudest words. Silences!
What children dancing by what fires
watching their shadows join with the flames?
If our children could know what we do to some children
they would never in their lives dance again.
They would throw over our furniture, heave their suppers to the floor.

In this state, nights clear through March and April turn pines fragile
with shrapnel shine exploding on this paper where I, brothers and sisters,
find myself frozen toward any hope letters will get through
so wrap up in my Social Security coat, father's dog tag over my heart,
to find with you through the frigid slush of our small
upriver city our legislative representatives' small
towering offices to beg in their absences for small willingnesses.

> Through artful lobby after lobby,
> we fight cold, wet feet
> seeking "windows of opportunity"
> where hardy rock-doves flock roof to roof
> in snaps of wrong-side-out covers being shaken
> in order to be cleansed.

➤

GARY WIDGER

Winter, 1939

The boot prints around the grave
are small German snow angels.

Today is a good day, because of the snow
falling and filling so we can pretend
the winter is done.

➤

KATE GEURKINK

Twilight's Last Gleaming

Snow crystals falling off hemlocks
The bright lights of shattering missiles.

Feeling the peace of deserted woods
Terror at the quiet before bombs fall.

Seeing the rockets' red glare
Now, the red and purple sunset.

Stars shine in the desert
They connect us in peace or in war.

Look up into that light and say
No more darkness, no more killing.

Stop the artillery that blocks
The light of the stars.

→→

MARION BUFFINGTON

Starry August

The late summer's night lay cavernous
between mountains, closed in original silence
before the world began. At the turn of the road,
composed of ancient earth, my whispered steps
among the spurting stones could not move, so awed
I was by the sudden stars filling the thick, hushed sky.
My arms became wings, and I gathered
the ecstatic night and the pop-out stars
until they pushed all wars away.

→→

HUGH HENNEDY

On Not Being Asked for a War Poem

WB having been asked wrote
He has had enough of meddling who can please
A young girl in the indolence of her youth
Or an old man upon a winter's night

Which isn't very far from WH's
Saying in his elegy for WB
That poetry making nothing happen
Survives in the valley of its saying

In the shadows of the ashen hollows of
Existence where now we are all called to serve
I not having been asked for war poetry
Nevertheless beat the ancient making drum

Young girls and old men in late summer and fall
In winter and spring and summer returned again
Old women and young men wherever we are in the cycle
Let us march to that which pleases and survives

➤➤

FRED SAMUELS

Prayer

Let Fear have no dominion in human hearts and minds,
for death will cleanse our wounds and pain and bring to rest
the tortured thoughts and strivings of the restless brain
and free the soul to harmonize with nature's best.
O ghostly atoms, gently recreate our Earth;
restore intrepid Hope to rightful place and worth!

Let Hate have no dominion in human hearts and minds:
as we are each a part of one and all, beware!
the wounds of hate infect the body politic;

its fever burns communal mind and breeds despair.
O gentle spirits, boldly recreate our Earth;
restore the Healer, Love, to rightful place and worth!

-><-

COLIN NEVINS

HUSHHHH

Many wonder if the waterfall speaks,

but poets know.

It speaks Hushhhh

no more guns

Hushhhh

no more bombs

Hushhh

no more cries of pain

Hushhhh

no more lies

Hushhhh

no more secrets,

as it chisels away

at our brainwashed minds.

-><-

In Heaven

Living at the edges, I grow stranger.

Heaven is here, I think, not there. There is no there there,
as Gertrude Stein said of her old hometown.

                          No congress of souls.
                          No fire and ice.

*

Two days after the autumn equinox,
                          last full week in September,

two cloudless nights under harvest moons,
                          the cinnamon fern turning brown,

the wind in the high canopy of our hundred year old oaks,
their still green leaves tossing and veering,
                          a foil of shining lit by the six o'clock sun.

*

Except for the persistent smack and wash and grind
of the Interstate,

we'd have no sense of the Empire,
                          its markets falling and wasted.

*

My neighbors' long-legged half-golden-retriever yaps happily
amid the red and golden delicious left to rot on sidewalk and lawn.

                          Bruised here. Worm-holed there.

Pecker-fretted and cidery. Nectar for marauding bees.

*

My president's a demagogue and a fool.
A man who's failed upward from privilege to privilege.
An expensive suit on a broken stick in an autumn field.

And so, this evening, my country stutters toward a war it doesn't want.

It wants this sweet wind.
It wants its sons and daughters alive and whole.
It wants a diplomacy elegant as wings.

Let the mullahs and CEO's
cry out in dust and blood.

This will still be the garden.
Its household gods the ant, the wood mouse, and the wren.
The trees its angels, engines of breath.

This last light slanting through shadow,
firing the red and orange of twiggy bittersweet in a milk glass vase,

the basket of red tomatoes,
the sullen unripe pears, green and blushing in their bowl,

                    will still stream and sing,

waste it how we will.

➤➤

L.R. BERGER

The President and the Poet Come to the Negotiating Table

I only agreed to compromise when it became clear
they were already stealing them again out from under us:
words, one at a time.

Okay, I said, like some ambassador for language
facing him hunched over my yellow pad of conditions.

He was wearing his orange tie and with the graciousness
of one who believes they have little to lose, he said,
There are far too many words, anyway.

Okay, then, I said, *you can have CONQUEST and DOW JONES.*
You can have BOMBS, but we want the SMART back.

This was fine with him. He had plenty of other words for SMART,
and would trade it for IMPERIAL and NUCLEAR.

TRADE is a word, I said, *you might as well keep,*
but don't touch SHADOW or PHENOMENA.

I gave up *SOFT* when paired with TARGETS
for the names of every bird. He said he'd consider
relinquishing CITIZEN for CUSTOMER.

I made my claim for CONSCIENCE, but he refused
until I sacrificed PERFECTION.

That's when he stood up shaking and wagging his finger at me.
He had spotted GOD upside-down on my list.

Under no circumstances, he said, *do you get GOD,*
and only calmed down when he heard me announce
I completely agreed with him.

GOD, I said, *must be returned to God.*

But this wasn't what he had in mind.
In his mind were SHOCK and AWE.

SHOCK was the word to bring me to my feet,
because poets can rise up angry and shaking
for what they love too.

SHOCK, I said. *You can have SHOCK.*
But AWE—over my dead body.

➤➤

MARTIN STEINGESSER

Those Pelicans

To Pablo Neruda, Santiago, Chile
September 23, 1973

Soldiers pacing the corridor
outside your hospital room:
a band of boots
                            to ring you out.
And you,
                lying there
drinking glucose in your veins,
plotting poems.
                        They know,
they know, those generals
itching to get you.
And you know what they won't forgive?
Joy! just as you said, on your words joy
came over to our side.

They say you wrote with a white mountain,
and while you sang a white star
circled above your hand
like a pelican bringing in the mail.
No one can stop them, Pablo—
                                    those pelicans
coming back and forth.

⇥

ROY GOODMAN

Pinochet Must Die

From where we stand,
perspective would lead the eye
across the plaza to the closed gray walls of the ministry.
But the eye is drawn to the solitary figure of a woman
dressed in a black skirt and black shoes
and a white blouse,

dancing—
one hand raised,
the other encircling the invisible waist
of the man whose photograph
is pinned to her sleeve.

The music is in her head, her heart—
she turns, she sways,
she steps lightly from square to square
never stepping on the lines
(like prison bars).

Her dance could conjure up the dead.
This defiant love could bring down castles.
She embraces what she has lost,
and all the world must tremble.

➤

MARTIN STEINGESSER

I Keep Thinking of You, Victor Jara

September 11, 1973

It's as if really I were there,
hearing the vowels of his red notes lift in the air
as big as blood oranges.
We are all still there, we are all arrested

in that night, filling the grandstands of Estadio Chile in Santiago
while the commandante mimics him, making motions as if strumming a guitar.
The soldiers want to put an end to such playing
and before us hold out his arms
and in two blows with an ax chop off the fingers of both hands.
Yet he stands up, and he sings —
                              we singing with him
until the stadium thickens with song like the voice of an army.
What could they do? What can soldiers do
after beating with rifle butts,
                              after cutting off fingers?

What could they do when singing, his singing went on
like fingers that go on playing without a hand,
like a heart that goes on beating without a body?
What could they do to silence him but shoot?

Victor, before you I swear
                              never to shut up.
I add this song to yours,
                              and curse you colonels of Chile, curse you

senators and presidents of death
                              with the fingers of Victor Jara.

➤

MARK SCHORR

Babii Yar Remembered

It has been too long since we talked
about the walk outside of Kiev called Babii Yar
the worst last resting place. But even
to imagine the worst was hard
without a sign or monument —
except for ravens circling the ditches,
kept in their scythed and bulldozed state,
where brigades moved and decisions were made.
I remember how you passed me on the path

until another man hobbled on to catch up.
Without saying anything, several of us
embraced as if to say, this is a century,
this is a place someone will try to wish away
unless we remember it here and mourn forever.

→►

Tom Chandler

For David Cicilline

Who would've thought that hope still has wings?
We've been told by the television that hope is a broken tower,
a broken airplane, the echoes of thousands of lost broken voices.
We've been told that hope is a tunnel now,
a hole of scumbled mud,
something we must crawl through on our knees.

We've been told by bloody headlines
that we're supposed to spend our lives as anxious shadows
and lock our doors and unlock our luggage and lock our hearts
and unlock our guns and lock our words, and lock our words.

And who would've thought on such a pale, shaken planet
that hope is still a bird with long strong wings
that rests its flight on the tips of buildings
and calls its name out over everything that's genuine and fair
and honest and fresh and rising up into a morning sky.

It took us all our lives to stand here at last
on the brink of the present, this tiny chip
of time we are sharing right now.

After all we've been through and before all that's just about to happen,
who would've thought that hope still has wings?

→►

A snowstorm hung on all of the afternoon
to fill the air and empty out the ground.
It hushed the walls that all had grief inside
and covered sidewalks that were open wounds,
as though this world of ours grew old and tired
and changed into another world, not ours.

Hope, I said to myself, this is despair
that walks us into darkness quietly
saying, you have a right to remain silent—
but I don't think I have. And now the snow
has stopped. What falls is never deep enough
to cover all our world. Hope is
and changes nothing but ourselves. So hope.

➵

ASKIA M. TOURÉ

A Few Words in Passing

The Ancients seem right; our common
delusions imprison us all—and our
world becomes, increasingly, a modern
Gulag. But, this is only a beginning:
how are we to find what truly matters?
We are indeed fortunate; we have
elders—Twa, Goggaju, !Kung—of our
Humanity; yogis, Sufis, lamas, babas,
zen masters, shamans, masters of
the Inner Realms. We must initiate
contact, seek them out, begin
the Soul's grand Dialogue with Self.
Perhaps the rainforests can aid us
on our paths; perhaps the mountains,
deserts, lakes, and the great oceans.
Perhaps the ants, dragonflies, butterflies,

perhaps our fellow mammals. ·
We must seek council with dolphins,
whales, the happy ones. Explain to
brilliant ravens, sad crows, immaculate
raptors. Begin rigorous chats with wolves,
bears, leopards, elk, rabbits and cats.
Fellow beings on our Great Maternal
Parent, Ile', the Earth; speaking deep
words, mirroring great truths, realigning
being, practicing harmony within realms
of Be/ing. My friend; when was your
last conversation with the rain?

➻

JAMES FOWLER

A Poem Made in the Shape of a Burning Buddhist Monk

In memory of Thich Quang Duc

This poem is made to be read aloud
on a crowded street and dropped,
with a match, into a beggar's bowl.

This poem will lift up in a cloud
of flames. High above, the fire
will burst and feather down upon
the shoulders of those pushing by.

There will be many poems read
in the memory of burning monks.
Tears will streak the sooty faces
of the ghosts. Ash will fill their cups.

➻

JEFF FRIEDMAN

J, the Chronicler

After the interrogations,
after the tortures,
after the streets were chalked
with the outlines of bodies

and the lines intersected,
crisscrossed
until they formed
yellow and white

constellations—
a broken Orion,
his trunk lopped
from his muscular legs,

the big dipper
pouring out particulate,
the twins grappling
twisting each other

to the point
where sinew snaps—
after the explosions
were cut off

from our hearing
and the small country
of our desire
burst into a beautiful

soundless blaze,
gold sparks
shooting from the blue
petals of flame,

after the last herd
of extinct animals
plunged into the fire
and only ashes swirled

from the ashes, I,
who knew nothing
of government or history,
who earned my living

at a small desk
under the humming
white tubes,
created a god

out of words and paper,
a god swooping
down from the clouds,
a whistle in flight

a god whose wings
spread open
like a Chinese fan –
huddled outside

under the dark sun,
those who could
no longer read
prayed,

and someone
with a spoon
and a wooden bowl
beat out of a song.

➤

S STEPHANIE

Tomorrow in the Apricots

Someone yells: When
will you love me?
Tomorrow in the apricots,
a small wind whistles
through the cracked mirror.

When will my ship come
in? Tomorrow
in the apricots,
the coin in the tin cup sings.

When will my stocks soar,
my health bloom, my name
ring out above this bloody war?
The starving cat cries:
Tomorrow, tomorrow!
Always tomorrow
in the apricots.

Tomorrow in the apricots,
tomorrow, when we
put out the flames of hell.

➜

WALTER RENTSCHLER

Tomahawks and Patriots

I believe the earth is flat,
hills and dales not withstanding,
and oceans flow over the edges
like waterfalls. I believe
Copernicus was all wet
and the sun really rotates around us.

I see it rise in the east and set
in the west and therefore the Church
should have stuck to its guns.
I believe world leaders also
think the world is flat—a big
playing board upon which chessmen
are moved to one square or another
to checkmate the rogue king. I believe
in tomahawks and patriots as they
once were, and I believe
in smoking the peace pipe before
throwing modern Tomahawks
and, unless we do, I believe
that some day we all
will be washed over the side.

→-

SUHEIR HAMMAD

What I Will

Humbly dedicated to June Jordan

I will not dance to your war drum.
I will not lend my soul nor my bones to your war drum.
I will not dance to your beating.
I know that beat. It is lifeless.
I know intimately that skin you are hitting.
It was alive once and hunted, stolen, stretched.

I will not dance to your drummed up war.
I will not pop spin break for you.
I will not hate for you or even hate you.
I will not kill for you.
Especially, I will not die for you.
I will not mourn the dead with murder nor suicide.

I will not side with you nor dance to bombs
just because everyone else is dancing.
Everyone can be wrong. Life is a right, not collateral or casual.
I will not forget where I come from.

I will craft my own drum. Gather my beloved near and our chanting
will be dancing. Our humming will be drumming. I will not be played.
I will not lend my name nor my rhythm to your beat. I will dance
and resist and dance and persist and dance. This heartbeat is louder
than death. Your war drum ain't louder than this breath.

➤

Patricia Frisella

Satyagraha

I will capture snowflakes with a horse's black eyelash
while your bombs scream into mud.

I will pick sun-warmed buttercups and strawberries
while rivers of warning flood your villages.

I will wear violet scarves and dance by moonlight
while your empires collapse, weighed down by gold.

I will eat apples and plums while your hunger
consumes you. I will know you with my eyes shut.

I will know that you sleep open-eyed, a saber
beneath your pillow. When you become ash

and brittle bone, I will be the wind whistling
through your skull and singing your name.

➤

SORLEY MACLEAN

The Cuillin

Beyond the lochs of the blood of the children of men,
beyond the frailty of the plain and the labor of the mountain,
beyond poverty, consumption, fever, agony,
beyond hardship, wrong, tyranny, distress,
beyond misery, despair, hatred, treachery,
beyond guilt and defilement; watchful,
heroic, the Cuillin is seen
rising on the other side of sorrow.

➤

CONTRIBUTORS

Contributors

LIZ AHL teaches poetry, creative writing, and women's studies at Plymouth State University, where she is a member of the English Department faculty. Her poems have appeared recently in the anthologies, *Mischief, Caprice, and Other Poetic Strategies* (Red Hen Press) and *Red, White, and Blues: Poets on the Promise of America* (University of Iowa Press), and in many literary journals, including *Crab Orchard Review, Prairie Schooner*, and *The Formalist*. She is a member of the Women of Words and lives in Bridgewater with thirteen antique typewriters. "Walter Cronkite Takes Off His Glasses" was inspired by a great American whose devotion to the truth and quiet humanity are sorely lacking in today's news media.

JOHN-MICHAEL ALBERT, born in OH, lived for thirty years in TX, and is currently a resident of Dover, NH. He is a published composer and has self-published three volumes of poetry, *Some Posthumous Thoughts of a New York Secretary, Texas Rose Rustler, and Boston Fruit Market*. He serves on the Board of the Poetry Society of New Hampshire, hosts and co-costs open-mike poetry readings, and can be found most evenings and weekends attending readings throughout NH's Seacoast. He currently supports his artistic avocation as an accountant in the Department of Music at UNH. John-Michael.Albert@comcast.net

BEVERLY STEWART ALMGREN retired in 1999 from a career as a college history teacher, mostly in Philadelphia, PA, at Moore College of Art and Design and The University of the Sciences in Philadelphia, primarily a technical school. Her specialty is Russian history, and she did several exchange programs in Russia during and since Communist times. She has written poetry occasionally since junior high, and since moving to Warner has intermittently enjoyed being part of several writing groups and programs.

BARBARA BALD'S passion for wilderness and animals led her to a career as a science educator, and to the riverside cabin where she lives part of the year without electricity or plumbing in the company of a dog, a cat and fish. For the past several summers she has attended the Frost Place Poetry Festival in Franconia, NH, and for the past several years she has practiced contemplative mediation. She dreams of swimming with manatees and visiting Alaska when brown bears are feeding on salmon. river1@worldpath.net.

PAUL BAMBERGER holds an MFA from UMass/Amherst. He is a Vietnam Veteran. He teaches ESL at Northern Essex Community College. pbamberger@necc .mass.edu

MEG BARDEN, now 87, has been demonstrating against war since she was 11 years old. She writes from an apartment in Keene and an 1830 farmhouse in Stoddard, NH. You can find her every Saturday 11 AM to noon at the Peace Vigil on Keene's Central Square. c/o vernadelauer@yahoo.com

KATE BARNES is the daughter of ME writers Elizabeth Coatsworth and Henry Beston. She lives on a farm in Appleton, ME which raises blueberries and hay. She has four grown children and lives alone with her cat. Until recently she drove her horse everywhere, but he is now 33 years old and happily retired. She has two books of poetry in print with David Godine, *Where the Deer Were* and *Kneeling Orion*. Her poems have appeared in such periodicals as *American Scholar, Kenyon Review* and *The New Yorker*.

MARYLIN LYTLE BARR celebrates publication of her most recent book of poetry, *Unexpected Light* (Essex Press, 1999) with readings in libraries and bookstores in MA, ME, and NY. Her original art is featured on the book jacket. (See Amazon .com)

TESS BAUMBERGER grew up on a family farm in SD, where she began writing poetry at the age of 11. She went to college in MA, stopped writing poetry, and spent the following 13 years as a research psychologist. She began writing again in 1998, as her career path took a big turn into parish ministry. She has self-published two books of poems, *As the Spirit Moves: Poems, Prayers, and Reflections* (2001) and *Green Leaves for Hair* (2003), the latter co-authored by Ralph Dranow. She has been featured at readings in the San Francisco Bay Area and in NH, where she currently serves a Unitarian Universalist congregation. She engages her progressive values as chair of the Public Policy Committee for the New Hampshire Council of Churches. Tess lives in Franklin with her ten year old son who lives to draw cartoon characters and bang on his drum set. poet_tess@verizon.net

GABRIEL FABIAN BAUTISTA is a Catholic priest and geographer from Buenos Aires, Argentina. In his doctoral thesis, *Intimacy with the natural world: a humanistic perspective*, he brought together his intellectual inquiries: poetry, society and nature, and religious beliefs. Now he is serving in a parish, working for the environment and strongly supporting The House of Poetry, a movement of poets from Buenos Aires.

L. R. BERGER's collection of poems, *The Unexpected Aviary* (Deerbrook Editions Press), received a 2003 Jane Kenyon Award for Outstanding Book of Poetry. She has been grateful recipient of awards from The National Endowment for the Arts, The NH Council on the Arts, The MacDowell Colony and was Visiting Artist at the American Academy in Rome. She works as a counselor, educator, and is New England Associate for *Pace e Bene,* an international nonviolence education service.

LAURE-ANNE BOSSELAAR is the author of *The Hour Between Dog and Wolf* and of *Small Gods of Grief*, winner of the Isabella Gardner Prize for Poetry for 2001. Her fourth anthology *Never Before: Poems About First Experiences* was published by Four Way books in 2005. She teaches a graduate poetry workshop at Sarah Lawrence College.

DEBORAH BROWN is a professor of English and chair of the Humanities Division at UNH in Manchester, NH. She lives on a former dairy farm in Warner, NH with her husband and cat. She has a chapbook, *News from the Grate* (Oyster River Press, 2002) and her poems have appeared in *Prairie Schooner, The Alaska Quarterly*, the *Beloit Poetry Journal* and others. She has poems and translations forthcoming in *Rattle* and *Smartish Pace*.

CICELY BUCKLEY has taught all ages, from 4th grade to adults, nature writing, French language and literature, and English as a second language. She came to editing early, and to Oyster River Press in 1989. Getting to know the American poets gives balance to her life shared with her sociologist and sax-playing husband on the upper Oyster River in Durham, NH.

DAVID BUDBILL's new book of poems, *While We've Still Got Feet*, was published by Copper Canyon Press in June of 2005. He is also the author of *Moment to Moment: Poems of a Mountain Recluse* (Copper Canyon Press, 1999). Garrison Keillor reads frequently from David's work on NPR's "The Writer's Almanac." David's most recent CD is, *Songs for a Suffering World: A Prayer for Peace, A Protest Against War*, with bassist William Parker and drummer Hamid Drake. He can also be heard on the CD *Zen Mountains-Zen Streets* with William Parker. David converted *Judevine*, his collected narrative poems, into a stage play which has now been produced more than 50 times in 23 states. The play is also the basis for an opera, *A Fleeting Animal* with music by Erik Neilsen. Recent interviews with David appear in *The Sun*, March 2004, in the Buddhist magazine *Inquiring Mind*, Fall 2004 and in *The River Reporter's Literary Gazette*, July 2005. David has been a freelance writer for 35 years. He lives in the mountains of northern VT. budbill@sover.net

MARION BUFFINGTON has worked with several non-profits including the New York Botanical Garden where she was assistant to the editor of *Garden Journal*. Before returning to NH, poetic leitmotifs sailing around her head prompted her to take a YWCA poetry writing class. Placing an article in New York's *Our Town* further encouraged her writing. She likes the surprise that a poem makes, carrying its own unexpected logic, and that poetry helps us endure the tragic, the injustice, the poignancy in human experience, while holding close life's tremendous beauty.

PRISCILLA BURLINGHAM began her artistic journey as a painter pointing to that which she found beautiful and important. Her painting led her to Yaddo and Ragdale where she first read her poems. At the millennium the poetry began to flow without pause, then poured after 9/11 becoming her major medium. "I write simultaneously about war, nature and sky in my studio on a New Hampshire pond and read all over New England in concerned venues. After this publication I plan to go to Mars via thought projection."

RICHARD CAMBRIDGE won the Master's Slam at the 1997 National Poetry Slam, and was a member of the 1992 Boston Championship Slam Team, and 3rd Place 1993 Cambridge Team. He has won the Allen Ginsberg Poetry Prize. His one-person theater piece, *The Cigarette Papers, A Spiritual Journey from Addiction* received wide acclaim and was described by the *Boston Globe* as a tour-de-force. He produced and co-authored *Where the Red Road Runs,* which ran for five months at Catch a Rising Star in Cambridge, MA. His current work is as co-founding member of Singing with the Enemy, a troupe of poets, musicians and performance artists. They brought their show !Embargo! To Havana, Cuba in 1998 for the first US–Cuba Friendship Conference.

MICHAEL CASEY of Lowell, MA, drafted into the Army in 1968, began his service as a military policeman, and spent much of his deployment on Highway 1 (QL 1) in Quang Ngai and Quang Tin Provinces, South Vietnam. His first book, *Obscenities,* recently reprinted by Carnegie Mellon, was in the 1972 *Yale Younger Poet Series,* edited by Stanley Kunitz, and went on to sell 100,000 copies in paperback. He has published four other books, most recently *Raiding a Whorehouse* (Adastra Press). He teaches creative writing at Northern Essex Community College.

MICKEY CESAR was born in upstate New York and lives in Lawrence, KS with an eighteen-pound tomcat named Alexander Nevsky. His book *Vanishing Point* was published by 219 Press of Perry, KS in 2005 and his poems have appeared in *I-70 Review, Coal City Review, Kiosk, Artwhore,* and *UnHoly Day Press.* He served in the U.S. Armed Forces as a sailor aboard a destroyer during Operation Desert Storm, and as a soldier during Operation Iraqi Freedom. He is now happily a civilian.

TOM CHANDLER is the Poet Laureate of Rhode Island. He has been named Phi Beta Kappa Poet at Brown University, and been a featured poet at the Robert Frost Homestead in NH. The author of four books, he is a columnist for *The Providence Journal* and editor of *The Bryant Literary Review.* He is professor of creative writing at Bryant University.

EDITH NEWLIN CHASE was born in a Quaker community and died in 2004 at the age of 99. She began writing poetry as a child, recording, while she was milking, her words with pencil stubs on tags from grain bags. She was a member of the Bank Street Writers Lab, where she began writing children's books, several of which, including *The New Baby Calf,* have been published separately as picture books.

DAVID CONNOLLY, born and raised in South Boston, served as an Infantry-man with the 11th Armored Cavalry Regiment in Vietnam from 68 to 69. He is a husband, father and a grandfather, a musician, a poet and a Cub Scout leader of Pack 210 in Southie. He holds a BA in English from UMass, Boston and was one of the founders and an original board member of the William Joiner Center for the Study of War and Its Social Consequences. Dave is widely published in journals and has his own collection of poetry and prose, *Lost in America*, which is about to be re-printed for the third time, as well as a new chapbook, *Finding My Way*. He is the managing and poetry editor of the *South Boston Literary Gazette*, the chairman of the South Boston Arts Association and the Slam Master of the monthly Southie Poetry Slam. Dave is one of the featured poets from the documentary *Voices in Wartime* which looks at how poets view and comment on war from Homer to the current conflicts. SouthiePoet@aol.com

ROBERT CORDING, professor of English and Creative Writing, is a poet in resi-dence at the College of the Holy Cross, MA. His fifth collection of poems will be out in Spring 2006. He has received two NEA fellowships. rcording@holycross .edu

YAMILÉ CRAVEN'S poems have appeared in *NH College Journal, Intense Experience* (UNH), *NH Magazine* and a variety of poetry anthologies. She has pub-lished four chapbooks. She has lived in Europe, Australia, the American South, and served in the WAC in DC and Frankfort, Germany. She runs an Email Poetry Workshop and has been a long-time member of the Poetry Society of NH. swiss4@ fcgnetworks.net

CURT CURTIN served in the US Army and the US Naval Air Reserve, and has worked as a Court Appointed Advocate for children in foster care, as director of a mental health agency, as a college teacher, as a dock worker and truck driver. He reads and listens to poetry among members and guests of the Worcester County Poetry Association. Most recently he was a featured reader at White House Poets in Limerick, County Limerick, Ireland, and has won the 2005 Jacob Knight Award for Poetry. curtinoconnor@charter.net

ROBERT DANA was recently appointed Poet Laureate of Iowa. His most recent books are *The Morning of the Red Admirals* (Anhinga Press, 2004), *Summer* (Anhin-ga Press, 2000) and *A Community of Writers: Paul Engle and the Iowa Writers' Work-shop* (University of Iowa Press, 1999). In the summer he works in his rose garden, wild flower garden and herb garden. In the winter he shovels snow. RPNDANA@ aol.com

THOMAS DIEGOLI is the son of a naval officer and a high school teacher. He grew up spending his summers in a tent in Conway, NH, on the Saco River, where he developed a love and respect for nature. After college he moved to the family farm in Chatham where he raised vegetables and sheep for 15 years. In 1990 he returned to the Mt. Washington Valley, married and raised three daughters. He has been an electrician, machinist, chef, cabinet maker, teacher, art dealer and picture framer. He has published two chapbooks, *One with the Land* and *Interface,* and a DVD, *The Skunkskin Session.* He is a NH Hunter Safety Instructor. thomasjdiegoli@earthlink.net

BILL DOLLOFF, a 48-year-old resident of Manchester, NH, grew up in VT and enlisted in the Marines in 1977. Throughout his life people have commented on his writing and imagination, but it was not until he retired from the Marines in 1999 that he took up writing. The somewhat contrasting image of a poetic Marine seems to surprise people. "I don't know why, Marines aren't all rough and tough." His topics include romance, war, love, loss, children and nature. waterway2@comcast.net

NANCY DONOVAN discovered Edgar Allen Poe living in a bookcase in her parents' home, and "Annabelle Lee" and "The Raven" became her favorite poems. In high school she read T.S. Eliot, Oscar Wilde and Francis Thompson. She chose a nursing career, and uses poetry to clarify her thoughts and feelings. Her only previous publication was a discussion of Aids, Ethics and Confidentiality in *The Journal of the National League for Nursing.* She lives in Hampton, NH. beachtreeattheC@comcast.net

ROBERT J. DUFFY is a plumber and pipefitter who lives in Franklin, NH, where he has raised four children in a small house overlooking the Winnepesaukee River. His work is a product of his life, but is not autobiographical. His collection, *Ordinary Lies,* was published in 2003 by Oyster River Press. He recently won second prize at the 2005 Austin International Poetry Festival.

ROBERT DUNN served as Portsmouth, NH's second Poet Laureate. He points out that Geoffrey Chaucer up and died in 1400, but we still hear from him now and again. Robert is somewhat younger.

DIANA DURHAM is the author of two books of poetry, and most recently the non-fiction *The Return of King Arthur* (Tarcher of Penguin, USA). Focusing on the power of the spoken word, she was a member of the London poetry performance group Angels of Fire. In NH she founded 3 Voices, a performance trio of women writers. She has lead poetry performance, writing, and storytelling workshops, most recently focusing on the meaning of King Arthur and the Quest for the Holy Grail myths in our lives. She is a graduate of University College of London, with a BA in English Literature. diana-durham@earthlink.net.

EUGENE ELANDER lives with his wife in Hillsboro, NH and Gotland, Sweden. Besides serving as adjunct economics faculty at Plymouth State University and Southern NH University, he has served as animal control officer for the town of

Farmington, NH. His book, *The Right Click* is a true tale, in verse, of love and romance which began over the Internet and ended in a marriage. A sequel, *The World Click*, co-authored with his wife, Birgit, will be published in 2006. He and his wife fostered a wolf hybrid that has moved on to the Loki Clan Wolf Refuge.

NEIL ENGLISH performs his poetry throughout NH, VT, ME and MA. His work has been included in several anthologies including *Portsmouth Unabridged: New Poems for an Old City*, *Entelechy International: A Journal of Contemporary Ideas*, and *Images From Ruin*. English has collaborated with former Portsmouth Poet Laureate Maren C. Tirabassi and humorist Rebecca Rule creating a spoken word Christmas CD *Sticky Mittens and Angel Feet*. He brings his enthusiasm for poetry to venues as varied as The Goffstown Women's Prison and schools from the elementary grades to the university level. Vice President of the Poetry Society of New Hampshire, Neil lives in Epsom with his wife and best friend, Leigh. There he maintains a modest collection of antique bricks imprinted with their maker's finger prints, the hoof prints of errant hogs and the intricate designs of the pitter-patter of eighteenth century showers petrified for all of time. neilinnh@usadatanet.net

ANNIE FARNSWORTH lives with her two children and an assortment of rescued critters under a grove of sheltering pines in southern ME. Annie is a metaphysician and works in a mental health facility, counseling patients in crisis. Her written work has appeared in various small-press journals and anthologies and she is the author of the chapbook, *Bodies of Water, Bodies of Light*. annie.farnsworth@verizon.net

JAMES FOWLER spent twenty-five years in the Navy based in Japan. In 1971, at Los Angeles Airport, anti-Vietnam demonstrators surrounded him, called him names, and spat on him. He resolved to stay out of the US and did so for ten years. He returned to attend to his dying father, then periodically to visit his aging mother. He returned permanently to study at Antioch and as a practicum edited *Heartbeat of New England: An Anthology of Contemporary Nature Poetry*, published by Tiger Moon Productions of India. He married, joined writers groups, and to supplement his pension teaches writing at the Village Square Booksellers in Bellows Falls, VT. When the US invaded Iraq he came full circle and joined the demonstrations against the war. He is a member of Poets Against the War and reads at antiwar poetry events. jfowler@fmis.net

LOIS FRANKENBERGER has worked with words in public relations since college. She has raised two prize-winning children, and began writing poetry when she was 60. Her poems have appeared in regional publications. A resident of Andover, MA, she is a member of Bartlet Street Poets and the Powow River Poets and is on the board of the Robert Frost Foundation.

JEFF FRIEDMAN is the author of four collections of poetry: *Black Threads, Taking Down the Angel, Scattering the Ashes*, and *The Record-Breaking Heat Wave*. His poems and translations have appeared in many literary magazines, including *American Poetry Review, Poetry, New England Review, Literary Imagination, The Forward* and *The New Republic*. He has won two fellowships from the New Hampshire State Arts Council, the Editor's Prize from *The Missouri Review* and the Milton Dorfman Poetry Prize. He is a core faculty member in the M.F.A. Program in Poetry Writing at New England College.

PATRICIA FRISELLA, the daughter of a decorated WWII combat vet who received his medals in November of 2001, lives with rescued horses on the side of a high hill surrounded by fields and forests and watched over by one of the few remaining manned fire-towers in NH. At night she can walk up the hill to see the lights of Newington, NH some 40 miles away or stand at the window and listen to owls and coyotes. She has won prizes for her short stories, essays, and poems, most recently the Anthony Piccione Memorial "Poets For Peace" Award. Her work has been published in various literary journals and anthologies. frisella@worldpath.net

KATE GEURKINK has been a nurse practitioner in women's health for over 20 years. She feels that a side effect of menopause was the desire to write poetry. Her poems have appeared in the *Dartmouth Medical Magazine* and in *The Pharos*. Her license plate reads SILWO for Silver Woman/Wolf. KATEG555@msn.com

ROBERT GIBBONS has published three full-length books of prose poems *Streets for Two Dancers* and *The Book of Assassinations,* both by Six Gallery Press, and *Body of Time*, Mise Publications, Pittsburgh. He is poetry and fiction editor of *Janus Head*, published biannually online and in print. He lives in Portland, ME with his wife Kathleen, also a writer.

ETHAN GILSDORF moved back to the States at the end of 2004, after five years in Paris, and now lives in the Boston area where he makes his living as a freelance journalist, poet, critic, editor and teacher. A Lee, NH native, Gilsdorf, 39, is the winner of the Hobblestock Peace Poetry Competition. He has been awarded a grant from the Vermont Arts Council (1999) and residencies at the Millay Colony (2005), the Hall Farm Center for Arts and Education (VT/USA, 2004), the New Pacific Studio (New Zealand, 2005–06) and Vermont Studio Center (VT/USA, 1999). His poems can be seen in *Poetry, The Southern Review, The North American Review, The Massachusetts Review,* and *Poetry London,* plus anthologies like *Short Fuse: The Global Anthology of New Fusion Poetry*; *Outsiders: Poems About Rebels, Exiles, and Renegades*; *Radio Waves: Poems Celebrating the Wireless*; and *In the Criminal's Cabinet*. Gilsdorf was the Paris regional coordinator for Poets For Peace/United Poets Coalition. ethan@ethangilsdorf.com

TESS GLYNN is a feminist, Buddhist, wife, mother and poet. Motherhood-font, source and protector of life defines her best. She believes we shape the future of the planet by the kind of care and guidance we give our young. Much of her poetry is defined by her passion for nurturing life, for peace, for overcoming struggle and illness, and just plain survival. She was one of the first poets to publish poems at the Poets against the War website, and her poems have appeared in other journals. mstgln@aol.com

ROY GOODMAN was born in South Africa, and moved to Israel in 1969 to study at Hebrew University in Jerusalem. He moved to the US in 1972. His writing is strongly influenced by what he saw during apartheid, during the first years of the occupation of Palestinian lands, and during the waning years of the Vietnam War. He has been a taxi driver, factory production worker, and director of operations in the high tech world. He has published a few poems on the Poets against the War website and in the British counterpart. He also has work published in the *2001 Anthology of New England Writers*. royg@aol.com

DAMON GRIFFIN has lived in VT, MA, ME and NH since his birth in 1986. He was part of the Walnut Hill Arts Creative Writing Department where he studied with Daniel Bosch. His work has been published in *The Blue Pencil* and *The Apprentice Writer*. He is attempting to build the largest collection of stills from Akira Kurasowa's films and wishes to find more. He is attending the University of Maine.

HANNELORE HAHN is a holocaust survivor; a translator of the scientific correspondence of Albert Einstein; an author of her memoir, *On the Way to Feed the Swans*, and the founder/executive director of the International Women's Writing Guild.

JACK HALEY served as a machine gunner with the First Battalion Ninth Marines in Vietnam until his entire unit was wiped out and he was medevacked and discharged. After PTSD returned him to the VA, he became an Outward Bound instructor focusing on Vietnam Veterans. He was introduced to poetry by Doug Anderson, poet and fellow veteran. He worked for eleven years with Ellen Watson editor of the *Massachusetts Review* (which has published his work) and director of the Poetry Center at Smith College. He now lives in Putney, VT with his two children and works with fellow poet and Veteran, Jim Fowler. He says the muse strikes him "when relief persistently refuses to come, when I'm not all gone but not quite all here . . . when I'm getting honest with myself." john.haley11@verizon.net

SIDNEY HALL, JR. has lived most of his life in southern NH. He is graduate of Reed College, where he studied Greek and Latin Classics. He has been a publisher, editor, columnist, Latin teacher, and conservationist. He is the owner of Hobblebush Books, and also specializes in fine book design and production for other publishers. His poems have appeared in the *Graham House Review, Chattahoochie Review, Hampden-Sydney Poetry Review, Wisconsin Review, Midwest Quar-*

terly, California Quarterly, Hollins Critic, the Los Angeles Times Book Review and other magazines, as well as on Garrison Keillor's *Writer's Almanac* and in several poetry anthologies. His book reviews have also appeared in the *Los Angeles Times Book Review*. He is the author of two books of poems, *What We Will Give Each Other*, and *Chebeague*, and a book of memoirs, *Small Town Tales*, a collection of newspaper columns. sidhall@charter.net

GERTRUDE HALSTEAD was born in Germany in 1916. She escaped to France during the war where she was interned at Camp Gurs in the south of France. She volunteered to work as an interpreter and subsequently was freed. She eventually made it to Portugal where she was able to get passage on the last ship leaving for the United States. She currently resides in Worcester, MA where she is a member of John Hodgen's writing workshop. Her work has appeared in *Sahara, Diner, VOX, Amoskeag, Surroundings East, Columbia Poetry Review* and others. Her first book will be published in 2006 by Adastra Press. She has twice been nominated for the Pushcart Prize. c/o seavoice@mac.com

WALID HAMED, the Desert Poet, a Palestinian living in East Jerusalem (Al Quds), was born in Haifa, and both his parents were born in Silwad (Ram Allah), in Palestine. He writes poems in both English and Arabic. His first poem, "My Mother Tongue" was dedicated to his mother, and written, in Arabic, upon her death. It was translated by him into English and Hebrew, and later translated by others into ten languages. Two of his poems have been set to music, "Stranger in the West" and "Shadow of Life." He is program coordinator for Seeds of Peace in Jerusalem, a program that brings young people from Palestine, Israel, Egypt, Jordan, Pakistan, and India to join each other and Americans at a summer camp in Maine. He offers special thanks to Anoek De Smet of Brussels, Belgium for help in revising his poem. walidhamed@gmail.com

SUHEIR HAMMAD is the author of *ZaatarDiva* by Cypher Books, as well as other books of poetry and prose. Her work has appeared in anthologies and journals, as well as on radio, television and stage. She is an original writer and cast member of the TONY award-winning Russell Simmons Presents Def Poetry Jam. www .SuheirHammad.com

JAMES F. HARRINGTON was born in Boston, MA and grew up in a Catholic, blue-collar, working-class family. He converted to Islam in 1999 after long struggles with depression. In 2000, he married, for the first time, Enayat Alzayat, originally from Syria. He is a member of Veterans of Conscience, Poets against the War, and the Communist Party of the USA. He supports all oppressed peoples in their struggle for human and economic equality. Prior to moving to TX, his NH license plate was "VIVA CHE." cosmos69@yahoo.com

HUGH HARTER is an internationally known scholar of Spanish and French literature whose bilingual editions of major poetical works, *Shadow of Paradise*, and *The Diary of a Newlywed Poet* by Nobel Poets Laureate Vicente Alexander and Juan Ramón Jiménez, are widely recognized as masterful. He has translated seven novels from the French. The books he has written include *Gertrudis Gómez de Avellaneda, Tangier and All That*, and, more recently, *Return to Patton's France, 1944's Odyssey Retraced*, and *The Countess*. Harter has BA and PhD degrees from Ohio State University, an MA from Mexico City College and a Doctor of Letters degree from Alma College. He was director of the Instituto Internacional in Madrid and founder-director of university programs in both Spain and France. He is listed in *Who's Who in America* and *in the World*. He is a veteran of World War II of Intelligence in Patton's Third Army. Harter and his wife Frances have traveled extensively and lived in Europe, Latin America, and North Africa. After years of maintaining a residence in New York City, they are now living in Portsmouth, NH. hharter@comcast.net

SAMUEL HAZO is the author of books of poetry, fiction, essays and plays, and he is the founder and director of the International Poetry Forum of Pittsburgh, PA. He is the McAnulty Distinguished Professor of English Emeritus of Duquesne University where he taught for 43 years. A National Book Award Finalist, he served as the first poet laureate of Pennsylvania. His recent book of poems, *Just Once: New and Previous Poems*, received the 2003 Maurice English Poetry Award, and his collection, *Flight to Elsewhere* was published in 2005. SAMHAZO1@earthlink.net

CJ HECK lives in NH with her husband. She has three daughters, five grandsons and one granddaughter. A published poet and children's author, (*Barking Spiders and Other Such Stuff*, July 2000), and a Vietnam War widow, CJ also writes fiction, non-fiction, essays, and poetry from her inner feminine side. Some of her work has been published by CTB/McGraw-Hill, Writers Digest Books, Little, Brown and Company, Oxford University Press, Dane Publishing House, Inc., National Wildlife Federation, St. Anthony Messenger Press. cjheck@barkingspiderspoetry.com

HUGH HENNEDY has published two books of poetry and his poems have appeared in many journals. Three of his poems are forthcoming in *Enopoetica*, a collection of poems concerned with wine. A New Englander by birth and inclination, he lives in Portsmouth, NH.

BURTON HERSH is widely published, and two of his biographies, one of Edward Kennedy and one on the Mellon Family were national best sellers. His book, *The Old Boys, the American Elite and the Origins of the C.I.A.*, was well-received by his colleagues in the Association of Former Intelligence Officers. His most recent novel, *The Nature of the Beast* was published by Tree Farm books, 2002. He is an avid writer and tennis player. bandehersh@aol.com

ELLEN HERSH'S poems and translations have appeared in reviews and anthologies, including *Ad Hoc Monadnock* and *Under the Legislature of Stars*. Ellen holds degrees from Radcliffe, Yale, and an MFA from Vermont College of Norwich University. She and her husband divide their time between St. Petersburg, FL and Bradford, NH, where invading field mice try to exercise guest prerogatives. bandehersh@aol.com

WILLIAM HEYEN lives in Brockport, New York. Among his books, *Noise in the Trees* was an American Library Association Book of the Year, *Crazy Horse in Stillness* won 1997's Small Press Book Award, and *Shoah Train: Poems* was a finalist for the National Book Award in 2004. He is the editor of *September 11, 2001: American Writers Respond* and other anthologies. Etruscan Press will publish a new collection, *The Confessions of Doc Williams & Other Poems*, in 2006. Most recently, he has written about a thousand 13-syllable poems, one of which, "Freak Chick," probably has to do with our being divided against ourselves: "Its two heads hated one another, / pecked four eyes dead." wheyen@rochester.rr.com

JERRY HICKS, an A.S.U alumnus, is a L.A. writer and photographer. His poetry has appeared widely, including in *Pearl, Rattle*, and *So Luminous are the Wildflowers*. Currently artist-in-residence at PoeticDiversity.com, he also teaches essay writing in an adult ESL program. Most recent book, *Stalking Oma's Daughter*. beach .poet@att.net

BURKHARD HOENE, raised in NH, graduated from UVM and began his career in fashion at Brooks Brothers. His poetic journal entries, accompanied by his photography, inspired many who knew him. He died in 2004 at the age of 46.

HILARY HOLLADAY is professor of English and director of the Jack and Stella Kerouac Center for American Studies at University of Massachusetts Lowell. Her poems have appeared in *Verse, Margie*, and *Literature and Belief*, among other publications. She is the author of a poetry chapbook, *Baptism in the Merrimack*, and her most recent scholarly publication is *Wild Blessings: The Poetry of Lucille Clifton* (LSU Press, 2004).

BARBARA HOMANS lives in an old farmhouse on a country road in Alstead, NH where she paints and writes poetry. The poem, "After the Bombardment" was predicted in a watercolor of the same name.

CYNTHIA HUNTINGTON'S latest poetry collection, *The Radiant*, winner of the Levis Prize, was published in 2003 by Four Way Books. Huntington is the author of two previous books of poetry: *The Fish-Wife*, and *We Have Gone to the Beach*, as well as a prose memoir, *The Salt House*. She has won numerous prizes and awards including two National Endowment for the Arts grants in poetry, and fellowships from the Fine Arts Work Center in Provincetown, the New Hampshire State

Council on the Arts, and the Massachusetts Artists Foundation. She is Professor of English at Dartmouth College and past Poet Laureate for the state of NH.

JIM IRONS hails from Twin Falls, ID, where he recently completed his duties as Poet Laureate for the state of Idaho. He is an associate professor of English at the College of Southern Idaho. A self-described "snobby" wine enthusiast, Irons also enjoys traveling and tiramisu.

ANNALIESE JAKIMIDES is delighted to report that she no longer pumps water by hand although she will always miss the way light savages a morning sky in Mt. Chase, ME. People are the reason she rises each morning and celebrates each day. Her poems, essays, and short stories continue to be published in magazines, journals, and anthologies, and broadcast on public radio. She lives in Bangor, ME. amamama@usa.net

ILYA KAMINSKY was born in Odessa, former Soviet Union in 1977, and arrived to the US in 1993, when his family was granted asylum by the American government. Ilya is the author of *Dancing In Odessa* (Tupelo Press, 2004) which won the American Academy of Arts and Letters' Metcalf Award, the Dorset Prize, and the Ruth Lilly Fellowship given annually by *Poetry* magazine. *Dancing In Odessa* was also named Best Poetry Book of the Year 2005 by *ForeWord Magazine*. Ilya also writes poetry in Russian. His work in that language was chosen for "Bunker Poetico" at Venice Biennial Festival in Italy. In late 1990s, he co-founded Poets For Peace, an organization which sponsors poetry readings in the US and abroad with a goal of supporting such relief organizations as Doctors Without Borders and Survivors International. He has served as a Writer in Residence at Phillips Exeter Academy and has taught poetry at numerous literary centers. Currently, he works as a Law Clerk at Bay Area Legal Aid, helping impoverished and homeless people solve their legal difficulties. He lives in Berkeley, CA with his beautiful wife, Katie Farris. ilya_kaminsky@yahoo.com

J. KATES is a poet and literary translator who lives in Fitzwilliam, NH. jkates@ worldpath.net

MAGGIE KEMP, MD, trained as a specialist in occupational and environmental medicine. A performance poet, she makes her home in Lempster, NH with her husband, two teenage children, and two dogs. She spends her free time writing, kayaking and watching the loons.

DON KIMBALL is a retired family therapist living in Concord, NH. His poetry has appeared in *The Formalist, The Lyric, Edge City Review, Iambs & Trochees*, and other journals. He has received Honorable Mentions in the Newburyport Arts Association Poetry contest 2004 and The Lyric Poetry Contest 2003. He is a member of the Powow River Poets of Newburyport, MA.

LESLEY KIMBALL is a recent recipient of a Voice and Vision Award, a collaborative public art project sponsored by the Portsmouth NH Poet Laureate Program. She is director of the Wiggin Memorial Library in Stratham, NH, where poems are handed out to the public every day.

BECCA KRASNER is an eternal college student. So far her secondary education has consisted of a year at an upper class, brick, east-coast college; a year in Paris; and a brief stint at cooking school. She had just begun to fear that her phenomenal Exeter education had spoiled college forever when she was struck with a sudden, burning desire to take a test, write an essay, and debate western social theory in a dining hall. Therefore, she is currently in the process of applying to college for the fourth (and hopefully final) time. She hopes to take the city of Boston by storm, resume her athletic career as a fencer, and avoid actual employment by making lots of money playing her bagpipes in the T. Her life revolves largely around a quest to find a decent source of French cheese in America; an obsession with hors-d'oeuvres; an undying love of anything involving words; and constant tending to the every whim of Zora, a small yellow cat, whose tail has fortunately not fallen off. ouibeque@gmail.com

MAXINE KUMIN'S fifteenth book, *Jack and Other New Poems*, was published in January 2005, following *Bringing Together: Uncollected Early Poems 1958–1988* and *The Long Marriage;* a memoir titled *Inside the Halo and Beyond: Anatomy of a Recovery;* and *Always Beginning: Essays on a Life in Poetry.* Her awards include the Poets' Prize, Ruth E. Lilly Poetry Prize, the Pulitzer Prize, and the Harvard Arts Medal. She and her husband live on a farm in NH.

DUDLEY LAUFMAN lives with Jacqueline in a cottage on the edge of the woods in Canterbury, NH. They earn their money playing fiddles for barn dances. He has been published in many journals and magazines and several collections from small presses including their own Wind In The Timothy Press. www.WindInTheTimothyPress.com

KATE LEIGH is an emerging poet published twice in local anthologies. Mother of four grown daughters, she is a massage therapist, aromatherapist, and nature lover. midhvn45@yahoo.com

MICHAEL MACKLIN works as a carpenter and lives with his wife, Donna, and half Lab-half Golden Retriever, Murphy, who is the most blissed-out muse possible. He refused induction in 1969 and would love the chance to refuse again. His chapbook, *Driftland*, was published by Moon Pie Press. He also serves as reviews editor for *The Café Review*. mmacklin@maine.rr.com.

SORLEY MACLEAN (Somhairle MacGill-Eain) was born at Osgaig on the island of Raasay on 26 October 1911. He studied English at Edinburgh University and then became a school-teacher in Skye, Mull and Edinburgh. He began to write while still a student and was an established literary figure by the end of the 1930's. During the war he served with the Signals and was wounded three times, seriously at El Alamein. He went back to teaching until 1956, and from then until his retirement in 1972 he was headmaster of Plockton Secondary School, Wester Ross. He received the Queen's Gold Medal for poetry in 1990. He saw fascism not only in Spain, not only in Nazism, but also in the Highlands at the time of the Clearances. Possibly his best-known single poem is *Hallaig* about a cleared village. His poetry gave Gaelic a 20th century voice, a voice which blazed with passion and raged with anger against the injustice to the Gaels: the Clearances, betrayal by those in power for the sake of their own greed and the contempt the civilized world held for the natural world and its indigenous people. He saw the Gaidhealtachd as a microcosm for the problems, cruelties and injustices of today's world. He died in 1996.

JUNE COLEMAN MAGRAB, born in NYC, raised in San Francisco, now lives part time in MD and part time in a seasonal cabin in NH. She is the recipient of several fellowships, including a MacDowell, and her work has been included in the Frost Place anthology, *The Breath of Parted Lips,* and several journals. The mother of two grown daughters, she lives with her husband, her dog, Gatsby, and her cat, Montana. junecoleman@earthlink.net

RODGER MARTIN'S attitude about war has been shaped by a mother who lived through the Blitz, a father who served in the 8th Air Force, an uncle killed in the Pacific, his own year in Vietnam as a combat engineer, and a youth split between England and the Amish country of PA. He edits *The Worcester Review* and is known best in China as a Monadnock Pastoral Poet with a new collection of poetry *On the Monadnock* coming out there in 2006. rmartin1@keene.edu

CLEOPATRA MATHIS' sixth book of poems, *White Sea,* was published in 2005 by Sarabande Books. Her recent book, *What to Tip the Boatman?,* won the Jane Kenyon Award for Outstanding Book of poems in 2001 from the New Hampshire Writers Project. Her work has appeared widely in journals and magazines, anthologies, and textbooks. She has been the recipient of many grants and awards, including two National Endowment for the Arts Awards, The Robert Frost Resident Poet Award, a Pushcart Prize, and the Peter Lavan Award for Younger Poets from the Academy of American Poets. Since 1982 she has directed the creative writing program at Dartmouth College, where she is the Frederick Sessions Beebe Professor of the Art of Writing.

SHELLEEN MCQUEEN moved to VT from Worcester, MA in 2003, leaving behind the "dog-eat-dog treadmillism" of her marketing consulting business. A goldsmith and "wearable wildlife" bead designer, McQueen views VT as the perfect place "to overcome life's undertow, commune with spirit, and create beauty." For McQueen, writing is a means of meditation, "a road map to inner wisdom;" and she titled a collection of short stories *Kittywhiskers,* because her totem, the mountain lion, "relies on its whiskers to navigate through life's process." Her poetry has been published in *Poetry Northwest* and in the chapbook *Four Star Poets* (Pentacle Press, Bellows Falls, VT).

DUNYA MIKHAIL is a well-known poet in her native Iraq. Her poetry is subversive, innovative and satirical. She is widely anthologized and has published several collections of poetry. In 2001 she received the UN Human Rights Award for Freedom of Writing. Her work, *The War Works Hard,* won PEN's translation award and was published by New Directions. She lives in MI and has one daughter. DMik139729@aol.com

COLIN NEVINS is 11 years old and has been studying Buddhism. He cares strongly about the issues that affect America, and how they will change his future, and poetry is a way for him to express his feelings. Although he worries that, because he is only a child, what he has to say won't change anything, he will continue to write, paint and express himself, and perhaps one day, put his thoughts into action. He has tremendous respect for those who are still fighting in a non-violent way for the ever-needed goal of peace. colin@mainstreetbookends.com

LEE NEWTON holds a B.A. from Bradley University and a M.F.A. from George Mason University. Twice nominated for a Pushcart Prize, he has received a fellowship from the Illinois Arts Council and a Lannan Fellowship from the Folger Shakespeare Library. He has won *Amaranth*'s Editor's Choice Award and been a finalist for the Charles Johnson Award in Poetry and the Virginia Down's Poetry Prize. His most recent creative and scholarly works have appeared in *Pleiades, Wisconsin Review, Lowell Review, Crab Orchard Review, Phoebe, Poem,* and the *Asian Pacific American Journal.* He is currently completing his manuscript *Everything Broken* and a play entitled *Hana.* He serves on the Editorial Advisory Board for *Collegiate English,* the Board of Directors for *Why Not Now?* (a non-profit organization dedicated to assisting disabled children and their families), and teaches creative writing, literature, composition, and Business Communication at Bradley University.

PAUL NICHOLS lives on a small subsistence farm in Loudon, NH with his wife, Mary. They have four grown children and four granddaughters. Paul served in Vietnam's I-Corps region with the Third Marine Division during 1966–1967. He regularly keeps a journal, writes poetry and essays mainly for therapeutic purposes though several of his works have been published. Paul twice returned to Vietnam during the 1990's.

AIRE CELESTE NORELL, a California native whose given name means, "wind in the heavens," is a contributing editor for the online litzine, *poeticdiversity*. She has performed her poetry widely in the Los Angeles area, and her work has appeared in

the *San Gabriel Valley Poetry Quarterly*, the *Messenger*, and the *Blue House*. vegan@
aireceleste.com

JULIA OLDER left behind the Vietnam War to live on the Golfo dei Poeti, Italy,
where she studied Dante and was mentored by poet Salvatore Quasimodo. She re-
turned to the nation's Capitol when it was ablaze with race riots and the assassina-
tions of the Kennedys and King. Again, she fled—this time on a writing fellowship
to Mexico. Residencies at Yaddo and The MacDowell Colony prompted her to find
a peaceful forest of her own in order to write full time. Since then she has published
two dozen books, including eight poetry collections, a verse play, fiction transla-
tions, and a novel and a companion anthology focusing on Celia Thaxter. .

PAT PARNELL of Stratham, NH, is author of two collections of poetry, *Snake
Woman and Other Explorations*, *Finding the Female in Divinity*, and *Talking with
Birches*, *Poems of Family and Everyday Life*. She and her husband, Bill, have made
their commitment to the future with eleven grandchildren and one great-grand-
child—may they live in a world at peace! patparnell@comcast.net

DAVID PELOQUIN is a writer, illustrator, internationally known folk musician,
and recording artist. His group, Compass Rose, performed at The Kennedy Center
for the Performing Arts in 2000. When not performing, he is working on a prose/
poetry autobiography, *Falling Up the Stairs Backwards*. He is the author of a poem
cycle entitled, *For a Moment, So Precious, I Stayed Awake*.

ANDREW PERIALE is a playwright, actor, and puppeteer. He is the founding
editor of *Puppetry International Magazine*, and, with his wife, Bonnie, designed the
Velcro® Puppet Playhouse line of toys. Each summer, he raises way too many to-
matoes, and makes enough pesto to last the winter. All things being equal, he'd
rather be in Italy.

JOHN PERRAULT practices law, sings ballads, and writes. His *Ballad of Louis
Wagner and Other New England Stories in Verse*, published by Peter Randall, is dis-
tributed by the University Press of New England. Individual poems have been pub-
lished widely. His recent collection, *Here Comes the Old Man Now* is published by
Oyster River Press. He served as Portsmouth Poet Laureate from 2003–2005. He
is available for performances and workshops through the NH Humanities Council
and the NH State Council on the Arts Touring Roster. www.johnperrault.com.

GAYLE PORTNOW divides her time between New York City and the fog of Cam-
den, ME. She photographs atmospheric conditions. Her Wheaten Terrier, Dudley,
makes her laugh and takes her walking. A discerning Bakelite collector, she wears
her 1930's and '40's plastic bangles even when writing at the computer. Her poems
have appeared in magazines including *Wolf Moon Press Journal*. gayleportnow@
yahoo.com

Patricia Smith Ranzoni, born in ME's Mt. Katahdin country, was the first woman from the northern chain invited to read her poetry at the annual Women of Appalachia conference, Ohio U. Zanesville. Living with dystonia, she is a disability rights activist. Puckerbrush Press published *Claiming* (1995) and *Settling* (2000). *Only Human, Poems From the Atlantic Flyway* is forthcoming from Sheltering Pines Press. In addition to writing from one of the subsistence farms of her youth, which her husband and children worked to help keep in the family, she is a master embroiderer and practitioner of homestead and woodland arts. pranzoni@aol.com

Walter Rentschler, a hospital executive for thirty years, took early retirement to play "Mr. Mom" for his two children by a second marriage. When not chauffeuring or attending to the many other demands of this enriching role, he has occupied his time collecting American art and English pottery along with gardening, hiking, and tennis. His interest in poetry began after hearing Billy Collins on NPR in 2002. He recently moved from NH to NC. wrrentschler@yahoo.com

Charles P. Ries lives in Milwaukee, WI. His work has been published widely and he has received three Pushcart nominations. He recently read his poetry on NPR's "Theme and Variations" program. His fifth book of poetry, *The Last Time*, is slated for publication later this year (Moon Press, Tuscon AZ). When not writing he likes to surf Lake Michigan year round with the Lake Shore Surf Club. charlesr@execpc.com

Eve Rifkah and her husband, Michael Milligan, are editors of *Diner*, a journal of poetry, and founders of Poetry Oasis, Inc., a non-profit poetry organization in Worcester, MA. She won the 2003 Revelever chapbook Contest with *At the Leprosarium*, a portrayal of the lives of the Peneikese Island Leper Hospital (MA) patients in the beginning of the 20th century. seavoice@mac.com

Connie Robillard is a Mental Health Counselor, specializing in working with those who have experienced trauma. She is founder of Eventide Counseling Services of Londonderry, NH. Her interest in mental health and the peace movement began in the 60's when friends returned from the Viet Nam war, changed. A close friend and artist was her first introduction to PTSD. "His presence and stories from the war, brought me to a new place in my own personal journey, social understanding and commitment to those who continue to experience the aftermath of traumatic events." Connie is an artist, co-author of a book: *Common Threads: Stories of Life After Trauma* which she wrote with co-therapist, Marcel A. Duclos. They are regular contributors to *Life Sherpa*, an online magazine. They are working on a second book and an artistic documentary on trauma and recovery. Connie, the mother of six children, is married to Paul Robillard; together they enjoy kayaking, working on their rustic house on a pond in southern NH and raising their youngest son, Mike. At last count they have 11 grandchildren with one more on the way. Connie is a member of the NH Mental Health Counselors Association, NBCC, USABP, NH Writers Project, Londonderry Artist Association. She is a workshop presenter and guest speaker.

DAVID ROMTVEDT was raised in southern AZ and that has shaped his life—a life lived on various margins. He served in the Peace Corps in Zaire and Rwanda and has worked as a carpenter on a sister city project in Jalapa, Nicaragua building a children's park and playground. He plays dance music of the Americas in the band The Fireants. His most recent book of poems is *Some Church* (Milkweed Editions, 2005). Romtvedt@wyoming.com

FREDERICK SAMUELS is a retired sociology professor. His book, *Intense Experience: Social Psychology through Poetry* (Oyster River Press, 1990) is a helpful tool in teaching social psychology. He has been writing poetry since age 11, and has been a long-time, active member of the Poetry Society of NH. His most recent book, co-authored by Joann Snow Duncanson, is *Breakfast in the Bathtub: A Book of Smiles* (Peter E Randall, 2005).

MARK SCHORR serves as Executive Director of the Robert Frost Foundation in Lawrence, MA. The poem included here is from his latest chapbook, *Various Ground Zeros*, a sequence of poems that bear witness to battlefields visited. markschorr@comcast.net.

PRISCILLA F. SEARS has been teaching English and Women's Studies for the MA:LS Program at Dartmouth since 1977. She has received many awards for her teaching. She has published two books, edited a third and has another forthcoming on her work in Bosnia after the recent war. She collects goddesses from the early Willendorf Venus to Marilyn Monroe. Priscilla.F.Sears@Dartmouth.edu

JANICE SMITH SEUFERT has lived many places, but returned with her family to her hometown in 1970. She lives on a high hill, where she is a naturalist and birder and often writes about rural life. She is a former president of the Poetry Society of NH, and former coordinator of the statewide children's poetry contest. nhpoet@hotmail.com

BAT-CHEN SHAHAK together with two friends was killed in a suicide bombing in Tel Aviv, Israel in 1996. She was 15 years old, and it was the Jewish holiday of Purim and the date of her birthday according to the Hebrew calendar. During the *shiva*, or week of mourning, Bat-Chen's family discovered that her diaries were filled with poems about peace. Her parents, Ayelet and Tzvika Shahak, became founding members of the Parents Circle-Families Forum (www.theparentscircle .org), a group of 500 Israeli and Palestinian families who have lost close members to the conflict and who call for reconciliation over retributive action. Bat-Chen's diaries have been published in Hebrew, Arabic, Italian, Dutch and Japanese and they are read by Jewish and Palestinian students in many schools in Israel. The Association for the Commemoration of Bat-Chen Shahak (www.batchen.co.il) was founded in 1997 to promote peace and literacy. Bat-Chen's poem "Three Shots" was written for Yitzhak Rabin, the Israeli Prime Minister assassinated by a right wing Israeli opposed to the peace process. His widow, Leah Rabin, said, "I would have loved to thank Bat-Chen for her striking, caring words in person. But I will never have that chance. Bat-Chen was killed in the terrorist bombing at Dizengoff Center in March, 1996, along with two of her girlfriends. Several weeks after the bombing, I visited the families of these three 15-year-old girls. Even after the devastating loss of his daughter, Bat-Chen's father had the courage to say, to me personally, and publicly on Israeli television, that he supported the peace process as passionately as his daughter had." ofri1@zahav.net.il

LEE SHARKEY is the author of *To A Vanished World*, a poem sequence in response to Roman Vishniac's photographs of Eastern European Jewry in the years preceding the Nazi Holocaust. She stands with Women in Black in Farmington, Maine, where she teaches women's studies at the university and edits the *Beloit Poetry Journal*. sharkey@maine.edu.

KATHERINE SOLOMON has an MFA in Writing from Vermont College and has taught at the NH Technical College in Claremont and Springfield College Extension in Manchester. Her poems have appeared in a number of journals and anthologies. She is the recipient of an Individual Artist Fellowship from the NHSCA for the year 2000, and has a chapbook, *Tempting Fate*, from Oyster River Press. She lives in Sutton, NH. k_solomon@mcttelecom.com

JOY STARR grew up in Washington, D.C. daughter of a retired Navy Captain and an accomplished painter. Reflecting her father's New England roots, she entered Wheaton College and heard Adrienne Rich, Richard Eberhart, Stephen Spender, e. e. cummings, and W. H. Auden. After graduation and a career in the Nation's Capital, she married, moved to a log cabin in Virginia suburbs, raised two sons, and became a freelance writer appearing in the *Christian Science Monitor*, *The Washington Post*, *New Hampshire Profiles* and elsewhere. After retirement to NH her works have appeared in *Random Acts of Poetry*, *The Poet's Touchstone*, and the *Portsmouth Herald*.

KEVIN STEIN is the author of seven books of poetry and criticism, most recently the collection of *American Ghost Roses* (University of Illinois Press, 2005). He is Poet Laureate of Illinois.

MARTIN STEINGESSER sometimes dances on stilts and presents and teaches poetry for adults and kids through ME's Touring Artist programs. "A burning, tender voice," Baron Wormser said of his book of poems, *Brothers of Morning*. Individual poems appear in a broad spectrum of publications, including *The Sun*,

Garrison Keillor's Writers Almanac, Tiferet Journal, and *The American Poetry Review*. His sweetheart says he makes the best damn sliced egg sandwiches in Maine. windspooning@yahoo.com

S STEPHANIE's poetry has appeared in magazines such as *Birmingham Poetry Review, Third Coast* and *The Sun*. Her chapbook *Throat* came out with Igneus Press in 2001. She edits the literary magazine *Crying Sky: Poetry and Conversation* with her husband, Walter Butts. She lives and works as a nurse in Manchester, NH.

CANDICE STOVER is a native of Mount Desert Island, ME whose teaching has bought her to Shanghai and New Zealand, as well as the Frost Place in Franconia, NH and the College of the Atlantic in Bar Harbor, ME. Her first collection of poems, *Holding Patterns,* was selected by Mary Oliver to receive the Maine Chapbook Prize. Through the Linc-Arts mentorship program she works with young writers, and she has facilitated a women's writing group since 1993.

SALLY SULLIVAN came from Iowa to live thirty years in New York City and then thirty years in the NH woods. She has studied poetry with Pat Fargnoli and with a writing group at the Brattleboro Senior Center.

ALDO TAMBELLINI was born in 1930 in Syracuse, NY to a Brazilian father and an Italian mother. As an infant, he was taken to Lucca, Tuscany, and at the age of 10 enrolled in Lucca's art school. His family survived the bombing of his neighborhood during WWII and experienced, first hand, the repression of the fascists and the terror of the Nazis in Italy. In 1946 he returned to the US, studied painting at Syracuse University and earned a masters in sculpture from Notre Dame. In NYC he pioneered Video Art and Multimedia performances and opened the Black Gate Theater which showed experimental films and radical plays, and was the first Electromedia Theater for multi-media performances and installations. For nearly a decade he was a Fellow at the Center for Advanced Visual Studies at MIT. His work has been translated into Russian, Italian and Sicilian. In 1998 he founded "The People's Poetry" in Cambridge, MA. He is a co-founder of the poetry collective, "Poets Against the Killing Fields." His most recent film, *Listen,* won first place at the New England Film Festival, October, 2005 in the Experimental Short by an Independent Film Maker category. ATambellini01@aol.com

RONALD STUART THOMAS worked as a vicar in the Church of Wales from 1936 until his retirement in 1978. His last parish, Aberdaron, was located on the tip of the remote Llyn Peninsula. The bleak Welsh landscape and the harsh life of the farmers who were his parishioners provided inspiration for much of his finest poetry. Although he wrote his poems in English, he was a great advocate of the Welsh language which he learned at the age of 30. He was a fervent supporter of Welsh nationalism and even condoned violent action against English-owned properties in Wales. In 1964 he was awarded the Queen's Gold Medal for poetry. In 1998 The

Manic Street Preachers reproduced his poem "Reflections" on the cover of their CD *This Is My Truth Tell Me Yours*. It was taken from his final collection *No Truce with the Furies*. In 1996 Thomas was nominated for the Nobel Prize for Literature. He died in 2000 at the age of 87.

ELIZABETH TIBBETTS' book *In the Well* won the Bluestem Poetry Award (Bluestem Press, 2003), and a chapbook *Perfect Selves* was published by Oyster River Press (2001). She works as a nurse, and lives in the small town of Hope, ME where she swims and writes as often as possible.

MAREN C. TIRABASSI, a poet and liturgical writer is the author or editor of eleven books and two spoken word CD's. New this year are *A DayBook for New Voices* and *Transgendering Faith*. She co-hosts a monthly radio program with humorist Rebecca Rule, and has served as Poet Laureate of Portsmouth, NH, editing during her tenure an anthology of poems of place, *Portsmouth Unabridged*. She travels widely to lead workshops and retreats, and when she is home spends unconscionable amounts of time with her dog, Shade. mctirabassi@hotmail.com

ASKIA TOURÉ is one of the founders of the Black Arts Movement. A resident of Boston, he is a member of "Poets Against the Killing Fields" and "Artists for Peace and Justice" of Greater Boston. During the Civil Rights Movement, he served with the Student Nonviolent Coordinating Committee and participated in the Atlanta Project of SNCC which helped forge the Black Power Movement. He has lectured internationally and has published works in reviews in France, Italy, India, China and the US. He won the 1989 American Book Award, and his most recent collection of verse, *Dawnsong!* won the American Literature Stephen Henderson Poetry Award. His work is found in reviews in France, Italy India, China, and the US.

KATHERINE TOWLER is the author of two novels, *Snow Island* and *Evening Ferry*. She has received fellowships from the NH State Council on the Arts and Phillips Exeter Academy, where she served as the George Bennett Fellow. She has decorated her house with a collection of over 100 salt and pepper shakers, and when she is not writing, she can be found bicycling the back roads of New England. She lives in Portsmouth, NH. www.katherinetowler.com

GEORGE V. VAN DEVENTER served with the Signal Corps in the US Army and has been a house painter, warehouse man, truck driver, school bus driver and dairy farmer. For seven years he was director of the Live Poets Society of Maine and worked extensively in the public schools to develop poetry writing workshops for the children there. He is the current editor of *Off the Coast*, journal of the Live Poets Society. His poems have been widely published. He is a member of the John Clare Society of England and North America. He enjoys singing choral music and lives with his wife in Bristol, ME. In 1996 he was one of the many who helped carry the Olympic torch from Los Angeles, CA to Atlanta, GA. arge109@midcoast.como

MARGARET BRITTON VAUGHN has been TN's poet laureate since 1993. She is affectionately known as a "Tennessippian" because she was born in Murfreesboro, TN, and spent part of her life in Gulfport, MS. Maggi got her writer's voice from listening to country music, especially during the Ryman Auditorium years. She is the author of *Grand Ole Saturday Nights*, *The Light in the Kitchen Window*, *Kin*, *Acres That Grow Stones*, *Life's Down to Old Women's Shoes*, *Bell Buckle Biscuits*, *The Birthday Dolly* (co-authored with Carole Knuth), *Foretasting Heaven: Talking to Twain at Quarry Farm*, *America Showing Her Colors in Black and White*, and *When the Great Ship Went Down*. The recipient of many awards and honors, Maggi is especially proud to have been the first poet to receive a fellowship from the Elmira College Center for Mark Twain Studies. She currently resides in Bell Buckle, TN.

MARJORY HEATH WENTWORTH was born in Lynn, MA. Educated at Mt. Holyoke College, she received her MA in English Literature and Creative Writing from NYU. Her poems have appeared in numerous books and magazines, and she has twice been nominated for The Pushcart Prize. *Nightjars*, a chapbook of her poems, was published by Laurel Publishing in 1995. *Noticing Eden*, a collection of poems, was published by Hub City Press in October 2003. She was appointed Poet Laureate of SC in 2003. She teaches poetry in "Expressions of Healing"—an arts and healing program for cancer patients and their families at Roper Hospital in Charleston, SC. She serves on the board of directors of the Low country Initiative for the Literary Arts (LILA) and the Poetry Society of SC. She reviews poetry and writes a poetry column fro the *Charlston Post and Courier*. She lives in Mt. Pleasant, SC with her husband Peter and their three sons. She works as a book publicist.

MIMI WHITE enjoys walking her dog to Rye Harbor, especially on mornings when the light is just breaking the horizon. She has two grown daughters, two sons-in-law and two grandchildren. When she can take the time, Mimi and her husband enjoy flyfishing remote rivers of the US. She is the current Portsmouth Poet Laureate. Watch for and participate in her project, *What is Home*.

GARY WIDGER is simply Gary Widger. His name is an adjective that describes itself. You have to get to know him. He lives and he writes. And he loves music. He plays the guitar. He breathes. He thinks too much. He hopes his tiny poem touches you: a poem that concerns itself with the sadness of war; of people hurting and being hurt. garwidge@yahoo.com

STEPHEN WING, after graduating from college in 1978, took to the highway. While on the road he self published a chapbook or so a year, mostly to give away to folks who gave him rides. In 1990 he married Dawn Aura and settled in Atlanta. Southeastern FRONT published the best of the chapbooks in *Four-Wheeler & Two-Legged: Poems* (1992). He self-published his collected hitchhiking poetry in *Crossing the Expressway: Poems from the Open Road* (2001), his spiritual testament. He now works as catalog editor and recycling coordinator at a metaphysical book wholesaler, New Leaf Distributing, and designs bumper stickers for Gaia-Love Graffiti. His latest project is *Last Testament: A Melodrama of the Post-Petroleum Age,* which will unfold in serial installments on the web. Visit him at www.gaialovegraffiti.com.

BARBARA WINSLOW is a fiction writer and a graduate of the Iowa Writers' Workshop. Her translation of Dunya Mikhail's *The War Works Hard* won a PEN prize for translation and is published by New Directions Publishing. She lives and works in Las Vegas.

ANNABELLE WINTERS aspires to write poems that people will want to recite in the shower. She lives in Boston where she makes quilts while sipping tea, competes in occasional triathlons and road races, and is learning to make everything in the kitchen and on the walls from scratch. Her work has been published in *168 Maga-zine* and *Centripetal.*

SHOLEH WOLPÉ is the author of *The Scar Saloon* (Red Hen Press, 2004) and has a CD by the same title. Her poems, translations and reviews have been published in many literary journals, periodicals and anthologies in the U.S., Canada and Europe, Middle East and Asia. She was born in Iran but spent most of her teen years in the Caribbean and Europe, ending up in the U.S. where she pursued Masters degrees in Radio-TV-Film (Northwestern University) and Public Health (Johns Hopkins University). Sholeh is the recipient of several awards for her poetry and is the director and host of *Poetry at the Loft . . . and more,* a successful cultural arts venue in Redlands, CA. She divides her time between Redlands and Los Angeles, CA.

Copyright Permissions

Grateful acknowledgement is made to the following authors and publishers for permission to reprint previously published material.

Berger, L. R., "The President and the Poet Come to the Negotiating Table," from *Shock and Awe: War on Words* by L. R. Berger (New Pacific Press, 2004) and *Peacework* (May 2003).

Bosselaar, Laure-Anne, "The Feather at Breendonk" and "Leek Street" from *The Hour Between Dog and Wolf*. Copyright © 1997 by Laure-Anne Bosselaar. Reprinted with the permission of BOA Editions, Ltd., www.BOAEditions.org.

Budbill, David, "April 3, 2003," from *While We've Still Got Feet*. Copyright © 2005 by David Budbill. Reprinted with the permission of Copper Canyon Press, PO Box 271, Port Townsend, WA 98368–0271.

Casey, Michael, "a bummer," from *Obscenities* by Michael Casey (first published by Yale Series of Younger Poets, ©1972, Yale University Press). Permission from Carnegie Mellon University Press (reprinted by CMUP, ©2002). "people parts" ©2005 by Michael Casey, reprinted by permission of the author.

Chase, Edith Newlin, "Peacemaking" is from *Twigs from My Tree* by Edith N. Chase, (William L Bauhan, 1984).

Cording, Robert, "Christmas Soccer Game" from *Southern Poetry Review* (Spring/Summer, 2005).

Dana, Robert, "In Heaven," *The Monthly Review* (2003).

Duffy, Robert J., "Heroes' Welcome" from *Ordinary Lies* (Oyster River Press, 2003).

Durham, Diana, "Colors of the Tiger," *To the End of the Night* by Diana Durham (Northwoods Press).

English, Neil, "Distant Whir," *Entelechy International: A Journal of Contemporary Ideas* (Fall, 2003).

Fowler, James, "Cyclorama" appeared under the title "War" in *Contemporary Haibun, Vol V* (Red Moon Press) and *tug of the current: The Red Moon Anthology of English Language Haiku 2004* (Red Moon Press).

Friedman, Jeff, "J, the Chronicler," *Under the Legislature of Stars* (Oyster River Press, 1999) and *Scattering the Ashes* by Jeff Friedman (Carnegie Mellon University Press, 1998). "Memorial," *The Forward*.

Frisella, Patricia, "Satyagraha," *In Posse Review* and *Small Spiral Notebook*.

Gibbons, Robert, "The First Snow of Winter," "Its Mission," "When Time Is No Solution," "To Breathe the Least Bit of Fresh Air," "Can you Get the Sense of the Weight of a Gun from the Movies?" *Body of Time* by Robert Gibbons (Mise Publications, 2004).

Haley, Jack, "I Fell in Love with a Woman of the Opposite Sex," *Massachusetts Review* (1995).

Hall, Sidney, Jr., "Imagine," *Poets Against the War,* ed. by Sam Hamill (Norton, 2003).

Heck, CJ, "Taps," included by invitation in *"The Taps Exhibit,"* The Taps Project, Arlington National Cemetery (May 29, 1999).

Holladay, Hilary, "Summer of Love," *The Offering* (UMass, Lowell).

Huntington, Cynthia, "The Invasion of Canada," © Cynthia Huntington 2003. By permission of Four Way Books. All rights reserved for *The Radiant.*

Jakimides, Annaliese, "From This September Day," *The Café Review* (Vol 16, 2005). "Reunion at the Vietnam Women's Memorial Dedication," *Beloit Poetry Journal* (Vol 53, No 2, 2003).

Kaminsky, Ilya, "Maestro," from *Dancing in Odessa* by Ilya Kaminsky (Tupelo Press).

Kates, J., "Rest 8.6.8.8.6" has been published in *The Florida Review* and in the anthology *The Practice of Peace* (Sherman Asher, 1998). "How Can There Be a War Going On," *Cyphers* (Ireland). "After One War," *The Lungfish Review* (1993).

Kimball, Lesley, "The Canvas of War," *Spotlight Magazine.*

Kumin, Maxine, "Please Pay Attention, the Ethics Have Changed," *American Poetry Review.* "Purgatory," Copyright © 1965 by Maxine Kumin, from *Selected Poems 1960–1990* by Maxine Kumin. Used by permission of W. W. Norton & Company, Inc.

MacLean, Sorley, "The Cuillin," *From Wood to Ridge* by Sorley MacLean, (Carcenet Press, Ltd, 1990).

Martin, Rodger, "Toes," *Love and Trouble: An Anthology of Teachers' Writing,* (Plymouth Writers Group, 2002).

Mathis, Cleopatra, "Mother's Day, 1993: Hearing We will Bomb Bosnia," *Guardian* (Sheep Meadow Press, 1995), "Cleopatra Theodos," *The Center for Cold Weather,* (Sheep Meadow Press, 1990).

Mikhail, Dunya, Translated by Elizabeth Winslow, "Inanna" from *The War Works Hard* © 1993, 1997, 2000, 2005 by Dunya Mikhail. Reprinted by permission of New Directions Publishing Corp.

Newton, Lee, "Why We Make Love," *Crab Orchard Review.*

Nichols, Paul, "No Fear," *The South Boston Literary Gazette* (Vol 14, 2005).

Older, Julia, "Czechoslovakia," *San Miguel Review* (Instituto Allende, Mexico). "Soundings," from *Rolling the Sun* by Julia Older (Appledore Books, 2005).

Peloquin, David, "Eulogy," *Method Madness* by David Peloquin (Write Design Publications, 2005). Reprinted by permission of the author.

Perrault, John, "Ashes to Ashes " from *Here Comes the Old Man Now* (Oyster River Press, 2005) first appeared in *Fosters Daily Democrat*.

Ranzoni, Patricia, "Hearings," previously published in *Pemmican,* and *Only Human, Poems from the Atlantic Flyway* (Sheltering Pines Press, 2005). Permission of the author.

Ries, Charles P., "A Perfect Order," *Poesy* and *Free Verse*.

Romtvedt, David, "Gone," *Cream City Review* and *Some Church* by David Romtvedt (Milkweed Editions, 2005), "The Bells of Balangiga," *Borderlands: Texas Poetry Review* and *Some Church* by David Romtvedt (Milkweed Editions, 2005).

Samuels, Fred, "Prayer" from *To Spade the Earth* by Fred Samuels (Free Flow Press, 1999).

Schorr, Mark, "Babii Yar Remembered," *Various Ground Zeros* by Mark Schorr.

Seufert, Janice Smith, "Child of Sudan," *The Poets Touchstone* (Poetry Society of New Hampshire, 2004).

Shahak, Bat-Chen, "A Summary of War and Peace," "A Dream of Peace," "Poem to Peace," "Three Shots, In Memory of Yitzhak Rabin," *Children Write for Peace* (Givat Haviva, 2000) and *Rabin—Our Life, His Legacy* (Putnam Pub Group, 1997)

Solomon, Katherine, "Pentagon Fantasy," *Color Wheel* (Winter/Spring, 2004).

Stein, Kevin, "First Day, Container Corporation of America, 1972" and "While I Burned the Autumn Garden," from *Chance Ransom: Poems*. Copyright 2000 by Kevin Stein. Used with permission of the University of Illinois Press.

Steingesser, Martin, "The Disappeared," "I Keep thinking of You, Victor Jara," and "Those Pelicans" from *Brothers of Morning* by Martin Steingesser (Deerbrook, 2002). Copyright © 2002 Martin Steingesser.

Thomas, RS, "Borders," *Collected Poems—1945–1990,* by RS Thomas (JM Dent, an imprint of Orion Publishing Group, 1993).

Vaughn, Margaret Britton, "Maneuvers," from *Kin* by Margaret Britton Vaughn (Bell Buckle Press, 1994).

Wentworth, Marjory Heath, "Linthong," *Peregrine Magazine* (Vol XV, 1996).

White, Mimi, "Zaydee's Short Career in the Army," *Poetry Magazine.*

Wing, Stephen, "The Money Missing from Our Paychecks," *Four Wheeler & Two Legged: Poems* (Southeastern Front, 1992).

Wolpé, Sholeh, "Jerusalem, Aug. 10, 2001," *Grain* (Canada) and *The Car Saloon* (Red Hen Press).

Index of Authors

❧

About the Cover Illustration

"Fingerprints," is by Hannelore Hahn, president
of the International Womens Writing Guild. It is a
photograph of the World Trade Center revolving
doors taken July 31, 2001.